THE MEASURE OF MAN

Books by JOSEPH WOOD KRUTCH:

Edgar Allen Poe
The Modern Temper
Five Masters
Experience and Art
Was Europe a Success?
The American Drama Since 1918
Samuel Johnson
Henry David Thoreau
The Twelve Seasons
Great American Nature Writing
The Desert Year
The Best of Two Worlds
Modernism in Modern Drama
The Measure of Man

THE MEASURE OF MAN

On Freedom, Human Values,
Survival and the Modern Temper

by

JOSEPH WOOD KRUTCH

ALVIN REDMAN LIMITED
LONDON

First Published by
ALVIN REDMAN LIMITED
4 FITZROY STREET, LONDON, W.1
1956

Made and printed in Great Britain by
D. R. HILLMAN & SONS, LIMITED
Frome

For
Charlie and Mary

ACKNOWLEDGMENTS

The author wishes to thank the following publishers, periodicals and individuals for permission to quote:

The American Academy of Arts and Sciences for a quotation from "Philosophical Implications of Physics" in its *Bulletin,* Vol. III, No. 5

The Cambridge University Press for quotation from *Mr. Tompkins Learns the Facts of Life* by George Gamow (copyright 1952)

The Columbia University Press for quotations from *Modern Science and Modern Man* by James B. Conant (copyright 1952)

Harper & Brothers for quotations from *Evolution in Action* by Julian Huxley (copyright 1953)

Henry Holt and Company, Inc., for quotation from *Spring Birth and Other Poems* by Mark Van Doren (copyright 1953)

The Nation for quotation from "Bridewell Revisited" by Edwin J. Lukas (copyright February 1949)

The Macmillan Company for quotation from *Walden Two* by B. F. Skinner (copyright 1948) and from *Collected Poems* by W. B. Yeats (copyright 1950)

Leslie A. White for quotation from the Journal of the American College of Dentists for March 1949

The god of galaxies has more to govern
Than the first men imagined, when one mountain
Trumpeted his anger, and one rainbow,
Red in the east, restored them to his love.
One earth it was, with big and lesser torches,
And stars by night for candles. And he spoke
To single persons, sitting in their tents. . . .

The god of galaxies—how shall we praise him?
For so we must, or wither. Yet what word
Of words? And where to send it, on which night
Of winter stars, of summer, or by autumn
In the first evening of the Pleiades?
The god of galaxies, of burning gases,
May have forgotten Leo and the Bull. . . .

A*

CONTENTS

THE MEASURE OF MAN

1

THE LOSS OF CONFIDENCE

In HISTORY as it comes to be written, there is usually some Spirit of the Age which historians can define, but the shape of things is seldom so clear to those who live them. To most thoughtful men it has generally seemed that theirs was an Age of Confusion, and to some greater or less extent we always belong to a lost generation. Things are never what they used to be, and while some are resigning themselves to disaster, there are always others quite sure that much better times are on the way.

In the Age of Faith not everybody believed in God, and even during the closing years of the eighteenth century there were those who looked on Progress with a jaundiced eye. In its own day the French Revolution was as variously interpreted as the Communist Revolution has been in ours—as enthusiastically hailed and almost, if not quite, as much hated and feared. Yet in the end, neither the good results nor the bad were so decisive as many expected them to be. The new world was less different from the old than was generally anticipated, and if any group has been justified by time, it is that which held only that human nature must continue to be much as it has always been.

All these are things which it would be well to bear in mind at the beginning of any attempt to assess a *modern temper*. Much that we think about ourselves is more closely paralleled by what other ages have thought about themselves than we usually realize. To say that to many the future looks dark because we have lost our faith or because forces beyond our control have been released into a world no longer manageable is only to say what has often been said.

Yet it is also true that the more excitable have sometimes been right. A really dark age did succeed the disintegration of the Roman Empire. A radically new world did begin when the Renaissance succeeded upon those High Middle Ages which, to a few historians, have seemed a peak of civilization. There is no a priori reason why the most dismal prophets of calamity may not possibly be right, why we may not be at the beginning of an age darker than that commonly called Dark. History is short, and there is no way we can know whether the calamities it records are the worst that are possible. Progress is not inevitable, disaster not impossible.

One thing, moreover, seems reasonably clear: our age has a heightened awareness of and an unusually deep preoccupation with those uneasy convictions which are to some extent characteristic of all times. Though it has been called, by those who anticipate history, "The Age of" many different things, none of the other labels is quite so inclusive or seems to fit quite so well as the familiar "Age of Anxiety."

Man is, to be sure, a worrying animal. To some extent he has always been "anxious." But it does appear that some sort of uneasiness is now more widely acknowledged and more variously explained than even the most skeptical observer would believe to be usual. Only the relatively few thoroughgoing Utopians seem to escape some sort of uneasiness, and it means something that what these Utopians rest their faith on—revolutionary political change and vast extensions of technological prowess—are among the very things which the anxious view with most anxiety. Few ages have been less sure, rightly or wrongly, that they know what to expect.

Not since the Middle Ages has eschatology—or how a world ends—been so popular a subject of discussion. Though some seem convinced that civilization will emerge perfected after a world-wide calamity, at least as many predict that it will soon disappear altogether. On one thing only is there almost universal agreement: things can't go on this way much longer.

At the very least, the comfortable conviction, dominant over two centuries, that everything would grow slowly better has disappeared almost completely, and we are again believers in catastrophe rather than evolution. Even the most extravagant of Communists insist that chaos must

17

precede Utopia, and they join eagerly with the pessimists to discuss the question of how a world ends.

Two world wars and more than one third of a century lie between the last days of the Age of Confidence and the present moment. Many of us still living can, nevertheless, remember what a very different world was like; and we are aware, as younger men cannot be, how drastic and all-pervasive the change has been. Had you told us in 1914 what men would be thinking, believing and expecting in 1954, we should have found it harder to believe than the fantastic predictions of George Orwell are now.

It so happens that H. G. Wells and Bernard Shaw died recently, and within a few years of each other. No two men writing in the English language—perhaps no two men writing in any language—had been so widely accepted by literate men as spokesmen for the last phase of the Age of Confidence. In curiously diverse but complementary ways, each had spent half a century telling the world that all was—or at least that all could be—well. Yet both died crying "Woe, woe" to the very people whom they had previously reassured. And the astonishing fact is that their complete reversal of opinion passed almost unnoticed. When each said, almost with his dying breath, "All is lost," the same public that had once accepted so trustingly their former assurances hardly noticed the about-face, because it had already been taken for granted that Shaw and Wells, like everybody else, had been compelled to make it.

In the case of Shaw it is easy to distinguish the successive phases of the transformation. Just after the turn of the century and at the time when he was still more orthodox Fabian than anything else, he wrote in *Major Barbara* a bouncing fable intended to demonstrate how inevitably and automatically an industrialized, capitalistic democracy would transform itself into a gentle, socialistic state, preserving all the virtues and abolishing all the defects of the England he knew. Scarcely more than a decade later, he admitted in *Heartbreak House* that the expected transformation was not taking place on schedule and urged on his fellow countrymen his new conviction that, instead of waiting for the dialectic process to work out its benevolent inevitabilities, they must either "learn navigation" or go on the rocks. Approximately a generation after that, *Back to Methuselah* took another step away from any optimism which could possibly be called easy. The contemporary human being, it told us, is not capable of "learning navigation." It would take any individual at least three hundred years to do so.

Thus Mr. Shaw informed us, successively and after the intervention of barely decent intervals: first, that all *would be* well; second, that all *might be made* well; and, third, that *nothing could possibly be* well unless man managed somehow to transcend all those human limitations which are symbolized by his unfortunate tendency to die not long after the expiration of the Biblical three score and ten. After this succession of retreats, it is not surprising to find him arriving finally at a position summed up in his reply to a visitor who had mentioned that one of Shaw's fellow playwrights in America was troubled about the state of the world. "Tell him not to worry. If, as I believe, man is about to destroy himself, he will be replaced by something better."

At every stage, the current conviction was represented as constituting some form of reasonable optimism. A good life for mankind will *begin* in perhaps a decade; it will be *achieved* in perhaps a generation; it cannot be *hoped for* until some age so distant that its place in time can be described only by the phrase "as far as thought can reach." This is "hope deferred" with a vengeance, hope deferred until hope itself becomes a grisly joke, offered in the inconceivably remote future and only to creatures who will not be men like ourselves, but "something better." In his early maturity Shaw ridiculed the Salvation Army and warned us to "Beware the man whose God is in the sky"; in his old age that is exactly where he placed the pie we were jokingly promised. For him, as for so many of his contemporaries, the vision of a "better world," which had once been so vivid, grew dimmer as the vision of the catastrophes which must precede it grew more and more clear.

The fact that the style and the mind of H. G. Wells were so much more prosaic and literal than Shaw's makes him, perhaps, an even better illustration of the typical course of the transformation by which early twentieth-century optimism was turned into mid-century despair. Both men began as more or less orthodox Fabian Socialists, but while Shaw always had mystical inclinations, Wells put his faith in technology, and the result was that their respective dreams of Utopia are comically unlike. Thus, while the Wellsian man of the future was happily engaged in pushing buttons and pulling levers, his Shavian counterpart in *Back to Methuselah* seemed to be inhabiting a country from which almost everything material had disappeared and which was thus returned to a sort of pastoral simplicity well suited to the tastes of the Ancients, who devoted themselves to contemplation rather than, like Wells's men, to the manipulation of super-gadgets. But even before Wells himself began to concern himself less and less with the mechanical wonders of the future as he imagined it, Aldous Huxley had transformed the Wellsian dream into that nightmare which, by the twenties, it was beginning to seem.

More significant is the fact that Wells and Shaw were more alike in their despairs than they had ever been in their hopes. The last of Wells's many prophecies was published by a newspaper syndicate very shortly before his death. He also cried "Woe, woe," predicting utter catastrophe as almost certain for the whole world and choosing phrases astonishingly like Shaw's when he spoke not only of the probability that man would "destroy himself," but also of the different creature which would replace him. Thus before they died, both the great popular educators of the English-speaking world did more than tell their pupils that unspeakable catastrophe lay just ahead: they also formally renounced the human race as a failure.

Whatever one may think of Shaw and Wells, either as artists or thinkers, their validity *as evidence* can hardly be questioned. They were neither cult leaders on the one hand, nor mere mass entertainers on the other. Their audience included almost the whole middle section of intelligent men, who must have found them to some considerable degree convincing. No doubt both their optimism and their pessimism were more clear-cut and positive than those of their readers. What they stated positively, these readers, after the usual fashion of readers, often accepted with no more than a "There may be something in it." But the curve of their thought and expectation corresponds to the curve of the general enlightened opinion. No two men could more truly represent the temper of their age. The collapse of their hopes summarizes the collapse of those world hopes which they represented.

What misapprehension, error, blindness or folly misled them? What is it that now seems clear, but which we and they failed to perceive only a generation ago?

Shall we say only that the mood of an age, like the mood of an individual, is merely the superficial by-product of its recent experience; that the early nineteenth century was confident because it had lived for several decades in peace and growing comfort, while the mid-twentieth century is anxious because it has gone through two wars, a depression and various revolutions? Or shall we assume that what we *thought* had some sort of direct relation to what happened—that we, with the best intentions in the world, *guided* ourselves toward a conviction of coming disaster?

To some degree this is what we must assume, unless we embrace in its simplest and most absolute form the conviction that either the dialectic of matter or some other form of Fate determines what will happen to us, while ideas, convictions and intentions are no more than phosphorescent epiphenomena which accompany the unfolding of Destiny. And if we do assume that what the world believed had some influence on what happened to it, then we ought to examine its most significant beliefs, asking ourselves as we go along what was wrong with them.

Very orthodox Communists and very orthodox Christians think they know already. The latter can sum it up very briefly by saying simply that we "forgot God." The Communists need a few more words, but not really very many. They tell us that though Wells, Shaw and most of their declared disciples called themselves Socialist in a sense which implies an acceptance of Marxian teachings, they did not really "understand Marxism." In the first place, they often forgot to take literally enough and absolutely enough the Marxian doctrine which asserts the decisive role played by the dialectic of matter. In the second place, they clung sentimentally to all sorts of bourgeois ideals and weakly supposed that history could fulfill herself without requiring that those who wished to co-operate should sacrifice anachronistic scruples concerning individual rights, the sense of fair play, and the essential evil of violence. Therefore, even as an attempt to control

it, their ideology was confused and timid. They pretended
to announce the future, but they were not wholeheartedly
with it. Those who have implicitly and completely accepted either Rome or Moscow see clearly what is happening and know what to think. Nothing which occurs
surprises them, and they know that in the long run everything will turn out as it should. Theoretically at least, they
have escaped from the Age of Anxiety and live again in
an Age of Confidence.

But those who have not undergone either of these two
conversions are puzzled and apprehensive. Either something *was* wrong in the thinking, or something *went*
wrong in the plans, and they are sure neither what it was
nor even which it was. Still less are they sure to what extent the errors are corrigible, the operational mistakes susceptible of rectification. And since they are not, as Wells
and Shaw were, on the point of death, they are less ready
merely to exclaim "All is lost" as they prepare to make
their exits.

Man has, after all, survived up to now. He was "good
enough," and he could learn quickly enough to achieve
at least the minimal degree of success necessary for continued existence. Though he was neither good enough
nor educable enough to create Utopia, many of us never
supposed that he was. But if it has at last become evident
that he is not even good enough to survive, that is quite
another matter. He was good enough to do so for many
thousands of years. He survived his first struggles with
animate and inanimate nature; he survived his diseases,
his wars, his social systems, his religions, and a series of

misconceptions which now seem to have been sometimes almost suicidal. What has made him in 1952 less fitted to survive than he was in 5000 B.C.?

There is, to be sure, one answer to that question currently familiar in one form or another. Reduced to its simplest terms, that answer is this: man's ingenuity has outrun his intelligence. He was good enough to survive in a simple, sparsely populated world, where he was neither powerful enough nor in sufficiently close contact with his neighbors to do them or himself fatal harm. He is not good enough to manage the more complicated and closely integrated world which he is, for the first time, powerful enough to destroy. He is, perhaps, no more prone to war than he used to be and no more inclined to commit other evil deeds. But a given amount of ill will or folly will go further than it used to. And what is so obviously true in connection with war is equally true in less spectacular affairs. The complexities of an industrial society make men more dependent on one another than they used to be, and the whole machinery of government is harder to handle. Wisdom and good will have either not increased at all or, in any event, have not kept pace with the necessity for them.

If we grant this familiar interpretation, then there are obviously at least a pair of alternatives to extinction. On the one hand we can say with Wells, "Let us get wise as soon as possible." On the other hand we could, of course, say with Thoreau, "Simplify."

If civilization is too complicated and there is no immediate prospect of our learning enough to manage it, we might suggest a reduction of that complexity. Instead of constantly seeking new sources of power, either in the oil of Arabia or in the interior of the atom, we might dispense with some of the sources we now have, and we might deliberately attempt to return to a political and social order which we would be capable of managing.

Our neighbors in different parts of the world were less a threat to us when we could not reach them and they could not reach us as readily as now—when, as a matter of fact, we could not even communicate with them, except after an interval of months. We would not need to be afraid of the Russians and they would not need to be afraid of us if we were as far away from each other as we used to be. In the thirteenth century, man was good enough at least to survive, and he would be good enough to survive now if things were as simple as they were then. We may think that we would hate to give up our "higher standard of living," but is that what we have really got— or is it only a higher standard of dying? What we ride toward at high speed may not be a more abundant life, but only a more spectacular death.

If you object that it would be as difficult to persuade mankind to simplify as it would be to make it wise, you may get from the enemies of complexity a grim answer. Events will not make man wise, but they may simplify him, willy-nilly. As a witticism current during the Second World War had it: "I don't know what will be the most important weapon in the next war, but I know what

will be the most important weapon in the war after that—
the bow and arrow." No one fought our most recent war
for the purpose of "reducing the standard of living," but
in all the countries involved, except the United States, it
was reduced. After the next world war, or at latest by the
time the next two or three are over, the reduction in complexity may be evident enough to the survivors. These
wars might not, as Wells suggested, reduce man to the
status of an extinct species, but they would very likely put
him back into a new Dark Age, and he would probably
be good enough to survive again in that environment, just
as he was good enough to survive in it once before. A
thousand years later, he might get another chance to try
an industrial as opposed to an agricultural society. And
if there is anything in the belief that he is getting better,
no matter how slowly, then he might, by that time, be capable of making a go of it. If not, time is long. Back he
would go again into something simple enough for him
to be able to manage.

Neither of these prospects—compulsory simplification
or the long wait while Creative Evolution produces something better than man—seems very cheerful to us poor
creatures of an hour. We may be pardoned if we cast
about for some *tertium quid* and if we accept it when
found, even though it should raise doubts concerning the
correctness of some of the fundamental assumptions of
recent enlightened thought. If such representatives of that
thought as Shaw and Wells were compelled to admit the
complete wrongness of their predictions, why should we

not wonder whether their premises may not have been equally erroneous?

Even in the depths of their disillusion, neither seems to have considered that possibility. Relatively early in their respective careers, one began to talk about "the race between education and catastrophe"; the other, to impart his suspicion that man was "not good enough." At the end, one said, "The race has been lost"; the other, "He turned out not to be." But Wells continued to assume that the whole trouble arose from the fact that man did not learn quickly enough; Shaw, that it was only because he did not change himself as rapidly as he should. But if man was becoming less and less capable of managing his affairs, coming to seem less and less likely to survive, the fault may possibly have been not with man as he is and ought to be, but with the Wellsian and Shavian man into which he was trying to turn himself.

In other words, perhaps modern ideas about man and the universe in which he lives failed of their purpose in exactly the same way that modern technology has failed—partially, at least—to produce that nearly universal peace, prosperity and plenty that were expected from it. We have engineered ourselves into a position where, for the first time in history, it has become possible for man to destroy his whole species. May we not at the same time have philosophized ourselves into a position where we are no longer able to manage successfully our mental and spiritual lives?

Few men would maintain that the failure of technology

to achieve everything expected of it is due exclusively to a failure to develop fast enough, and not at all to the fact that it has often developed in the wrong direction—producing, for example, instruments of destruction more efficient than any of the instruments which foster and provide for a more abundant life. May it not be that in some fashion roughly analogous, we have educated ourselves out of certain ideas necessary to our survival, and that modern thought, like modern technology, has been busy chiefly with the preparation of instruments for an efficient as well as spectacular spiritual suicide calculated to occur at about the same time that the physical world is destroyed?

Nothing would have more greatly surprised the earliest modernists—say, the men of the Renaissance, if one wants to go back that far—than to learn that man was losing confidence in himself. In its early beginning, this modernism was the product of an upward surge of confidence in the capacities of the human being. It began by assuring him that he was capable of more than he had formerly believed possible; that he need no longer remain mentally limited by the horizon fixed in divine revelation, or physically limited by those forces of nature to which he was compelled to submit. He could stand on his own feet, determine his own destiny, and become like a god. Wells was still thinking in those terms when he used *Men Like Gods* as the title of a book. But his last apocalyptic eschatological vision was of this "God self-slain on his own strange altar"—the altar of technological achievement.

That paradox has been generally recognized and most

assiduously examined, but it has not been resolved. Behind it is another, less often discussed; and it may be that in this other lies the key to the first. What has been lost step by step is not only the conviction that we will manage to our own advantage the new world we have learned to create, but also the confidence in our ability to govern even ourselves. The fact that the same premises that attributed new potentialities to man soon began to deprive him of other supposed attributes and powers passed almost unnoticed, until at last we began to perceive how much less, as well as how much more, than he had formerly been the human being was now beginning to seem.

At least in many philosophies, as well as many theologies, he had been endowed with both Free Will and the ability to recognize certain absolutes called Good and Evil. It made comparatively little difference whether it was God or Nature, in the eighteenth-century use of the term, on whose permanent, accessible criteria he could rely. In either case he could know what he ought to choose or do, and it rested with himself to decide whether or not he would do it. He was not, as the modern man has come to believe, merely the product of the forces that have operated upon him. He could make value judgments in the validity of which he truly believed, instead of telling himself that if one thing seems preferable to another, it can be only because the interests or the traditions of our nation, our society or our class make it seem so. And we can hardly be expected to manage the machines that we have created when we no longer believe that we have the power either of making ultimate decisions or of knowing what ultimate decisions ought to be made.

Though many have tried, no one has ever yet explained away the decisive fact that science, which can do so much, cannot decide what it ought to do, and that the power which it confers must be guided by something outside it, if power is not to become—as it is already becoming— an end as well as a means. Yet it is just at this moment, when choices have become unprecedentedly fateful (because intentions can now be implemented as never before in the history of mankind), that scientific theories have persuaded us to abandon the very premises which might have made us feel capable of directing the power that science has put into our hands. If in one sense man is now more like a god than he ever was before, he has in another sense become less godlike than he ever previously imagined himself to be. The attributes of a god must include not merely power itself, but also the knowledge of how power should be used. What we have fallen victim to is thus not so much technology itself as the philosophy that has grown with its growing.

It is true that neither Shaw nor Wells was a fanatical exponent of this view which makes man not the captain of his soul, but the product of the forces that operate upon him. Shaw, especially, was prone to indulge an odd inconsistency when he alternately defended economic determinism and the theory that the will and imagination of the individual are all-important. Undoubtedly he was aware of the dangers inherent in too absolute an affirmation of what his Marxism seemed to imply. But the man whom he and Wells, each in his own way, were trying to educate was a man already prone to accept that very restricted estimate of his powers of self-direction that materialistic rationalism had encouraged. Hence the man whom both finally pronounced a failure was the man who had himself come to believe what that rationalism described.

To entertain the possibility that the creature who has become "not good enough to survive" is not man himself but only that version of man that he has recently accepted is not, necessarily, to assume that his thinking is either demonstrably or even actually false. Possibly, at least, his theories about his own nature are both correct and fatal. The atom bomb is no less a threat to the very people who made it because the revolutionary theory of matter in accordance with which it was designed is presumably true. Conceivably, we may be on the point of achieving spiritual as well as physical suicide because we have learned more than is good for us about both physical and human nature.

There remains, nevertheless, the cheerful possibility that we actually know less about the Science of Man than we do of the less difficult sciences of matter and that we may, just in time, learn more. Perhaps Hamlet was nearer right than Pavlov. Perhaps the exclamation "How like a god!" is actually more appropriate than "How like a dog! How like a rat! How like a machine!" Perhaps we have been deluded by the fact that the methods employed for the study of man have been for the most part those originally devised for the study of machines or the study of rats, and are capable, therefore, of detecting and measuring only those characteristics which the three do have in common. But we have already gone a long way on the contrary assumption, and we take it more completely for granted than we sometimes realize. The road back is not an easy one.

2

GRAND STRATEGY

Man has never seen very far ahead and perhaps he never will. He did not anticipate the real consequences of mechanical invention and he foresaw even less to what his intellectual processes would lead him. But when we look back from the vantage point of a later time we seem to perceive a sort of Grand Strategy. The steam engine seems to have been invented to make the industrial revolution possible; certain ideas seem to have been propagated to give social development a certain direction. And if we submit to this illusion it must seem that the Grand Strategy of nineteenth-century thought had as its aim the destruction of man's former belief in his own autonomy.

Long before that century began certain preliminary steps had already been taken. Some would put them as far back as the sixteenth when Copernicus jolted us out of our simple assumption that the universe of which we were the center might reasonably be supposed to have in us its purpose and its explanation. Others, to whom the Copernican revolution seems less decisive than it must have seemed to many in its day, would credit the succeeding century with the first important phases of the slowly evolving Master Plan.

They would say that when Thomas Hobbes proposed to explain human conduct as a mere branch of animal behavior he took the first step;·and that when Descartes undertook to describe the animal as a mere machine he took the second. In the synthesis which presently took place Descartes' refusal to include man among the animals was quickly forgotten and the lines of future development were laid down. Hobbes proves that man is an animal; Descartes proves that an animal is a machine. By a quasi-algebraical process one needs only to eliminate the term common to the two equations in order to get what by now most men seem to believe: Man is a machine.

Against this conclusion the eighteenth century struggled hard. For "God" it substituted "Nature," and its Deism, however shadowy it may now seem, forbade it to assume that either man or his fellow creatures were merely mechanical. It now saw Man as a creature "darkly wise and rudely great" and if God no longer clearly revealed his intentions, Man was nevertheless born with a brain which was not quite the blank slate of Hobbes because Nature had inscribed on it, before his birth, those outlines of her general principles which, as Pope has said, "touched but faintly, are drawn right."

Thus, if neither God's word nor the individual con-

35

science was any longer a sure guide, the voice of Nature still was. Man was not a machine and he was not a creature to whom Good and Evil or Right and Wrong were merely the conventions, the mores, of his society. Nature afforded him "at least a glimmering light," something outside himself which he might stumblingly follow.

Yet before the nineteenth century was half over this compromise was already too old-fashioned to seem tenable, and the Strategy developed into its mature phase. During that century three inclusive new hypotheses—each in its own way as revolutionary as Copernicanism and each destined to affect as profoundly man's sense of his relation to the universe—achieved wide popular as well as professional acceptance. They were, of course, Evolution, Marxism, and the Freudian psychology.

These three theories are not directly connected with one another. They cover somewhat different fields, they overlap considerably, and at points they are mutually exclusive. Any one of them may be accepted without implying an acceptance of the others and it would be difficult if not impossible to be an orthodox believer in all three. Yet they do have, nevertheless, certain important characteristics in common and each did in its own way contribute to the accomplishment of the Grand Strategy's purpose. Each emphasized the extent to which the human being is the product of forces outside his control.

From one point of view it makes very little difference whether we are told by Darwin that natural selection, operating with mechanical inevitability, has caused man to evolve from other forms of life; by Marx that we are the product of a society which is, in its turn, inevitably produced by the dialectic processes of matter; or by Freud that what we call our unique self is actually the result of the way in which the fixed "drives" of human nature have been modified by the things which have happened to us— especially by things which happened in an infancy now almost completely forgotten.

No matter to which of the three we listen with conviction, the result is to drift toward the assumption that we neither can nor need to do much of anything for ourselves. Throughout all time either natural selection has performed for us the function of what used to be called "aspiration," or the dialectic of matter has similarly performed the function of effort. Simultaneously the dominance of the unconscious motive has made it useless for us even to attempt to follow the ancient injunction: Know Thyself—at least without the aid of experts hired to know ourselves for us.

Disputes still rage concerning what each of the three great teachers "really meant." Freudians, for instance, sometimes assume that analysis releases freedom. But there can be no doubt about the fact that all three of the great teachers have been popularly interpreted in the fashion suggested. At worst each could be and has been made the excuse for a sort of secular Calvinism in the light of which man is seen as the victim of an absolute predestination.

At the very least and even when attempts have been made to explain away what seem the most obvious deductions, the effect has been to focus our attention on that part of ourselves over which we have least control. To science, especially when uninfluenced by Jung and Freud, the theories opened new fields of investigation into "the mechanical operations of the spirit" while they left everything not mechanical as mysterious as it was before. And scientists suffer from the effects of a human weakness from which science itself is theoretically exempt. Like ordinary men they tend unconsciously to assume that the phenomena with which they deal are more important and more real than those whose manifestations elude them; hence man himself began to seem more and more merely mechanical just because the mechanical aspects of his behavior were those most easily studied. Having begun with the legitimate purpose of discovering how much of human behavior could be accounted for in terms of physical law and animal psychology both literature and science now began, first, to answer "Nearly all" and then to disregard even the reservation implied in the "nearly."

Thus to accept the hypotheses of Darwin, of Marx and of Freud, to accept any one of them as even a partial account of the how and why of man's past development and future destiny, meant to emphasize strongly if not exclusively the extent to which he has played a passive role and to encourage him to see himself as essentially not merely a "product" but also a victim. To that extent all three encouraged what may be called "philosophies of exculpation." If Darwin seemed to deprive man of all credit for the upward evolution of himself as an organism, Marx and Freud seemed to relieve him of all blame for his sins and his crimes as well as for his follies.

Perhaps, indeed, we would not so readily have accepted the role of victim had it not been for the absolution which was offered in exchange for our surrender of importance and dignity. If there is a sense in which our teachers tell us that we cannot possibly succeed because, at best, we are only the lucky product of natural selection, fortunate infantile experiences, or a favored position in the social system, so, in the same sense, we cannot ourselves be failures. We many shift the blame for all that we have done or left undone upon the unfavorable environment, sociological or psychological, to which we were exposed. If there is some uneasy sense that our own shortcomings do really exist, we make even of them a sort of virtue when we permit them to function as the driving force behind a criticism of our social class, our nation, or the world at large upon which we thus unload any residual sense of personal responsibility.

Since dogmas do not have to be accepted in their full dogmatic rigidity in order to have a very powerful effect, the question of how clearly and how absolutely deterministic theories are held is of relatively little importance. What is important is the evident fact that educational, sociological, and even criminological principles and methods have come increasingly to focus attention and effort on that aspect of man and his behavior which seems most easily interpreted in accordance with such theories, so that even when man is not openly proclaimed to be no more than a "product" of "conditions" he is treated as though he were.

Educators, sociologists, and lawmakers have begun to act as though man were absolutely incapable of choice, of self-determination, or of any autonomous activity. The man they have in mind when they describe their principles, plan their societies, or draw up their codes is something significantly, perhaps fatally, different from any creature who could possibly escape the catastrophe which many formerly confident "engineers" have now begun to predict.

Moreover and merely by being treated as though he could do nothing for himself man is, perhaps, actually becoming less capable of doing so. Any society which not merely tells its members that they are automata but also treats them as though they were, runs the risk of becoming a society in which human capacities atrophy because they are less and less rewarded, or even tolerated, as well as less and less acknowledged.

As the individual becomes, either in theory or in fact, less capable of doing anything for himself the question what may be *done to him* inevitably comes to seem more and more interesting. If he is so much the product of his environment that neither spontaneously nor as the result of moral adjuration can his own will make effective decisions, then it seems to follow—not that he must be simply abandoned to evolution, the dialectic of matter, or the obscure workings of the unconscious mind—but that he may be reached indirectly through the manipulation of that total environment of which he is the product. Thus sociology begins to promise to achieve by scientific methods all that which religion and moral philosophy, proceeding on false assumptions, failed to accomplish.

In its mildest and most defensible form the result of this conviction is simply the whole broad, benevolent effort of social reformers to relieve poverty, provide opportunities for education, and remove as far as possible all obviously corrupting features from the environment in which the individual grows to maturity. Such merely pragmatic enterprises do not depend logically on anything more than a recognition of external influences as a factor in determining human fate and they do not demand for their justification any affirmation that human conduct or character is "nothing but" the product of the influences brought to bear upon the individual. Thus when Bernard Shaw declares that "the only trouble with the poor is poverty" his rhetoric may seem to imply an absolute determinism but, as his own writing makes clear, all he really meant to say was only that poverty is the factor which society can most easily control.

Unfortunately, however, working principles, especially when they seem actually to work, have a tendency to harden into exclusive dogmas. The fanatical contention that man is nothing but the product of his environment arises naturally in certain minds, and soon leads to the equally fanatical conviction that this same man is also limitlessly plastic. Though he cannot change himself at

B*   41 all, he may, nevertheless, be changed in any direction and to any extent. To the aspiring "human engineer" very heady possibilities seem then to open.

To him it seems that since man is a kind of machine there ought to be possible a Science of Man as exact and as effective as any other science which deals, as a Science of Man would deal, with the behavior of matter operating in accordance with known or knowable laws. Moreover, as the nineteenth century came so clearly to understand, such sciences reach their maturity when phenomena can demonstrably be both predicted and controlled.

These two last are, to be sure, not quite the same thing, and the second is subject to limits somewhat more narrow than the first: Astronomy can, for example, predict eclipses with great accuracy though it cannot at all control them. But the two are very often related and the aim of the Science of Man would be completely achieved when it became capable, first, of saying in advance what a human being would do and, second, within limits as wide as those within which the physical scientist works, of directing and manipulating the materials with which it deals.

Ultimately, of course, such a Science of Man would find itself faced, just as the sciences of matter already have been, with a corollary problem. It too would sometimes be compelled to ask not merely "how can this or that be done" but also whether, in some sense with which science itself seems unable to deal, we "ought" or "ought not" to do it. But this problem does not arise in the infancy of any science. The professor of the new Science of Man tends to think of himself as pure scientist rather than as educator or reformer. His only concern is to discover the methods by means of which prediction and control become possible.

In relatively crude and simple ways the social worker, the teacher, and the businessman are already using—often for simple and limited purposes—the methods, often crudely empiric, from the results of which the aspiring Science of Man begins to draw theoretical general conclusions in much the same way that the earliest theoretical physicists utilized the experience of mechanics and military engineers. The mental test, the aptitude test, and the sampling technique are increasingly used to discover in advance what candidate will be elected, what radio program will prove popular, what advertising slogans effective, what course of instruction popular. And in so far as the methods are successful in achieving their immediate purposes they encourage, if they do not actually fully justify, the assumption that human behavior is predictable because, like the behavior of material particles, it follows inviolable laws.

In similar rough and ready ways the technician interested in results rather than in general theories has also been learning more and more how to control as well as merely to predict opinions and tastes, not only by advertising campaigns and other methods of propaganda but also by the stress put upon certain ideals or activities in the schools. Even in the realm of the popular arts com-

43

mercial exploiters speak frankly of "making" a star or a song hit rather than of "discovering" him or it. They have their methods and the methods very frequently work. When the beginnings of popularity are detected, its full flowering can be directed and controlled.

Inevitably each success strengthens confidence in the soundness of the theory on which the enterprise was based. Human behavior must be predictable because it has been correctly predicted. Opinions, tastes, preferences, and actions must be controllable because they have been controlled. That being the case, there seems no reason why we should stop with random and piecemeal enterprises. Why should we not found all ethics and all aesthetics on what we know of man's predictable behavior, all education and government on what we know of the methods by which he may be conditioned? We have, it is said, found out at last both why so called "human nature" is what it is and how it may be made into something else. We have now only to decide what people ought to be like and how we want them to behave. After that it is only a problem in engineering.

The more advanced theoreticians have already reached this point in the formulation of their ultimate aims. No longer concerned exclusively with the specific details of this or that specific evil or ill, they are already looking forward to the time when not only society but human nature itself will be completely remade. As the Dean of the Humanities at the Massachusetts Institute of Technology told the Convocation of 1949, we must now recognize our "approaching scientific ability to control men's thoughts with precision." It so happened that Mr. Winston Churchill was an honored guest on the occasion of the Dean's address and he remarked in reply that he would "be very content to be dead before that happens." But Mr. Churchill is a conservative who has been accused of finding "brave" an adjective more appropriate to the old world than the new and, whether he likes it or not, he has lingered on into a society that is moving in the direction which seemed to him utterly horrible and which is also already pragmatically committed to theories the full implications of which it does not always face squarely.

In the course of this discussion we shall presently have occasion to undertake some analysis of the scientific and philosophical assumptions behind the new Science of Man as they are stated and defended by those who, up to the limit of their very considerable powers, do seriously attempt to face squarely all their implications. For the moment, however, we may return to the subject of things as they already are rather than things as they may some time be, and consider the significance of certain actual practices analogous on a somewhat higher level to the pragmatic use by politicians and merchants of the techniques already devised to predict and control public reaction.

Inevitably the opinions and attitudes of both the public and such of its leaders as operate on a level of critical awareness above that of those whom they lead, have been profoundly influenced by the practical success which pre-

dictors and controllers have achieved and by the general
if vague assumption that all men are primarily either victims or at least products of the conditions to which they
have been subject. An assumption of this sort is a com-
monplace in those popular psychological and sociological
disquisitions which fill the magazines as well as the "fea-
ture" pages of the daily papers and which have completely
taken the place of the sermonizings which were once
equally ubiquitous. What is more important, both law
and education have followed suit, and in the name of
what are perversely called "humane" attitudes tend to
treat the average man as though he were, indeed, the helpless creature implied by Marx or Freud and described in
naturalistic fiction.

Thus the education which is offered man comes more
and more to be thought of in terms of "adjusting" or "conditioning" him to predetermined opinions or attitudes;
and educational theory tends to be based more and more
on the Pavlovian assumption that something should be
done to him in much the same way that something is
done to a monkey being taught tricks or a dog trained to
bark and bite on the proper occasions. In a similar fashion
"social legislation," which professes the intention to do
him good, decides what he ought to have and then gives
it to him, disregarding both the fact that he may want
something else and that it might be more in accord with
the best kind of human nature if he were permitted to get
it for himself. Criminology—again in the name of a "humanity" which begins by depriving the criminal of all

human attributes—proceeds on the assumption that those guilty of "antisocial conduct" have been in no way responsible for that conduct and that they are most likely to be redeemed if they are first told that they, like everybody else, are mere victims of their experiences, and then promised that they will be reconditioned. Thus—and again in the name of humanity—it assumes that to urge him to be a man and to choose good rather than evil would be both unscientific and inhumane.

Even in the nursery we begin the process of explaining to the man-to-be that any faults he may exhibit are not actually his—and therefore possibly corrigible by himself—but only the result of some defect in his training or his environment. On the radio one may hear preadolescent participants in the junior forums assuring one another that when other children are what used to be called "naughty" that is "only their way of showing that they need more love," and thus from their tenderest age the future citizens are taught the art of exculpation and conditioned to believe that nothing but conditioning is important.

The question is not whether deterministic theories are to some extent true. No doubt some "naughtiness" in adults as well as in children is partly attributable to what has been done to them. But the important question is whether or not it is always and entirely such and, whether, if it is not, a mistake is made when we fail to recognize and promote whatever autonomous powers a human being may have. Certainly in the case of adults and to some lesser extent in the case of children there is another side to the truth: "Human beings should be loved." It is: "Human beings should be lovable." Even in the nursery it might be just as well if both sides of this truth were acknowledged. Already eight-year-olds, having spilled the ink, broken the Ming vase and pulled the cat's tail are leaping up and down in an agony of self-righteousness as they scream, "I want to be loved." It is unnecessarily hard to love them.

In the adult world the parallel is the criminal who knows too well what the criminologists very properly admit: namely, that society is sometimes partly responsible for crimes. This truth is properly employed when it helps us to understand and perhaps to forgive someone else. It is not properly used to forgive ourselves either too much or too easily. Many a malefactor comes into court already convinced that he cannot justly be blamed for whatever he did. But sometimes, perhaps, the real culprit is not so much society as it is the conviction that society must be to blame. Those who are too thoroughly conditioned to assume that only conditioning counts are very badly conditioned indeed.

Moreover the implicit assumption that only "conditioning" counts is not always permitted to remain merely implicit and even on the level of popular discourse the bolder sociologists sometimes permit themselves to state it as an inflexible dogma. Thus Mr. Edwin J. Lukas, Executive Director of the Society for the Prevention of Crime, recently wrote as follows in an important national weekly magazine: "In today's thinking anti-social behavior is considered to be the product of unique economic, sociological, and psychological factors in each offender's past history."

From this beautifully clear and unqualified statement several startling facts emerge. In the first place, of course, it assumes that neither Wickedness nor (even) Crime is a reality, since both are redefined as "antisocial conduct." Moreover, as the result of this redefinition it becomes obvious that every individual, in so far as he remains an individual, exists in a moral vacuum so that Robinson Crusoe ceased to be either a good or bad man while on his island because he lived in no society and his conduct could not possibly be either social or antisocial. In the second place the redefinition not only gets rid of such theological concepts as Original Sin and the Reality of Evil but also of every vestige of any implied possibility that there is anything in man which is to any degree self-determining, or that he can possibly be anything more than the result of the forces which have impinged upon him. All men therefore are entirely innocent. Their exculpation is complete. But to accept pardon they must also admit that they are absolutely helpless.

Among psychologists, especially when they are concerned with the child, one may observe even more exalted states of fanatical exaltation. Thus Brock Chisholm, head of the World Health Organization, finds a publication as

49

respectable as *Science* glad to publish his article on the causes of war, in the course of which he expresses the opinion that human aggressiveness is the result of a hatred of ourselves, arising out of the fact that we have sometimes been told that we were bad. "Babies need, not just want but need, uncritical love, love whose manifestations are quite independent of the babies' behavior." Given enough "uncritical love" they will grow up free from any "conviction of sin" and therefore free of aggressive tendencies.

It may seem strange that an age which has been on the whole rather too ready to explain human behavior by analogies with that of the lower animals and decidedly adverse to admitting any fundamental distinction between animal nature and human should be so ready, in a case like this, to overlook the suggestive fact that aggressiveness manifests itself at very low levels of animal life, even among creatures who have little or no parental care and so can hardly have had any conviction of sin instilled into them. In the light of that fact it might seem reasonable to suppose that aggressiveness, instead of being the artifical product of too little "uncritical love," arises out of impulses pretty deeply implanted in living creatures; that if, in the case of man, it is not the result of "Original Sin," then it must at least be a part of his animal heritage.

Nevertheless Mr. Chisholm is doing no more than making explicit and unqualified certain notions congenial to a whole school of influential psychologists and he is willing to abandon the whole, otherwise much favored, device of animal analogy if by so doing he can emphasize still more strongly the guiltlessness and the helplessness of the individual human being, who is now invited to imitate the too advanced child in the nursery and to excuse even his "antisocial behavior" as the result of the too little "uncritical love" which has fallen to his lot.

As in so many other instances, the most "advanced" view thus neatly reverses a previous conception. The "conviction of sin" which was once supposed to be a necessary preliminary to the first step in the direction of virtue becomes, instead, the source of evil. Men who say, "We have done those things which we ought not to have done and left undone those which we ought to have done," will hate themselves and, hating themselves, they will join others to launch wars of aggression, while those who have been taught to believe that they have no power over their own actions will live in peace with their neighbors. Stripped of its modern jargon Mr. Chisholm's position seems to be essentially that of what used to be called "philosophical anarchy." Men become criminals only because laws exist and wicked only because moral precepts have been taught. Confession, instead of being good for the soul, is poison.

Perhaps comparatively few people are ready yet to subscribe without reserve to this dogma when it is so nakedly stated but it is the ultimate logical conclusion from the less obviously absurd premises which they do accept and the only escape from it lies in some qualification imposed upon the premises at some lower stage of development.

Anyone who really accepts what the head of the Society for the Prevention of Crime calls "today's thinking" will find himself compelled to say to his children, or to any other young people whom he may be called on to advise, something like this:

"Some day the time may come when you will have an opportunity to murder your grandmother and to steal her purse. Do not, if that time comes, be foolish or unenlightened. In the first place murdering one's grandmother is now called "antisocial conduct"—which doesn't sound so bad. But that is not the real point. The real point is that if you tried to resist temptation, even if you merely tried to summon prudence, you would only be calling on consciousness for aid which consciousness, being an epiphenomenon, is powerless to give. Be modern! Stand quietly by until the event informs you whether or not the 'unique economic, sociological, and psychological factors' in your past history have determined that you will or will not hit the old lady over the head with an ax."

Most people will agree that this will hardly do. Some, even among the sturdiest upholders of "conditioning" as the ultimate cause of everything, will probably admit that being taught to believe in the impossibility of choice is, itself, a conditioning factor. They may even admit that the concept of moral responsibility is a sometimes useful illusion.

No doubt our ancestors had too much faith in the sufficiency of moral injunctions. No doubt they were too much inclined to bid children be good and adults law-abiding. They needed a Burns to remind them how

> What's done we partly may compute,
> But know not what's resisted,

though even Burns, who lived too early to meet "today's thinking," seems to assume that some resistance is possible. When Bernard Shaw, as already quoted, asserts roundly that "the only trouble with the poor is poverty" or Anatole France celebrates the impartiality of the law by remarking that rich and poor alike are forbidden to steal bread or to sleep under the bridges, each supplies a useful corrective to an exclusively moralistic approach. But what is genuinely an extenuating circumstance is not necessarily an all-sufficient and irresistible cause.

It seems quite obvious that the complete rejection of the concept of human responsibility and of all belief in the human being's ability to do anything for himself is pragmatically impossible. A society which consistently acted on the unqualified assumption that no one could be held in any sense responsible for himself or his acts is unthinkable, and if all contrary assumptions are really based on an illusion, then that illusion is indispensable both to the life of the individual and to the life of the social organism of which he is a part.

If the social and psychological sciences, which increasingly assert either that they are demonstrating the externally determined character of all acts, opinions, and tastes or at the least that we should assume for practical purposes that they are determined, are making claims supported by the facts, then the truth which they have discovered is, literally, a deadly truth. It is something which man cannot afford to know because he can neither know nor even believe it without ceasing to be Man and making way for that something, either better or worse, which the more apocalyptically inclined occasionally predict.

3

IGNOBLE UTOPIAS

T HAT exponent of "today's thinking" whose
opinion was quoted in the preceding chapter had not carried his own thought beyond the point where it was still
possible to accomplish a simple *reductio ad absurdum* and
to declare that his premises lead to principles pragmatically absurd.

Other social scientists and experimental psychologists,
operating on a different level, have proceeded further.
Some, like Professor Thomas D. Eliot of Northwestern
University, undertake the difficult task of explaining how
a man may be in some sense *responsible* for what he does
without actually being free to do anything else. In a paper
called "Social Control of International Aggressions" published recently in the *American Journal of Sociology* Professor Eliot says: "The basic fallacy lies in imputing to
offenders spontaneous, 'willing' evil and hatred and therefore treating them not merely *as accountable for their
acts,* but as personally guilty. Blame and guilt are very

actual feelings, *but they derive from false premises.* An enlarged perspective would show the offense and the offender emerging as parts of a larger situation-process, in which the offended community also provides the essential milieu and both are injured parties." (Italics mine)

Now this is a version of "today's thinking" considerably subtler than that previously quoted. But it poses a dilemma of its own. In former days those who revolted against the logic of Calvinism refused to accept the conclusion that an individual was responsible and punishable for doing what God had predestined him to do. Professor Eliot appears to have embraced a secular version of this same theology when he distinguishes between what men may be *held accountable for* and what they may be *blamed with.*

Other thinkers concerned less with such immediate matters as national or individual criminality adopt even more radical attitudes toward the question of man's nature and the kind of future to be hoped for him. Many of them are well aware that their convictions imply changes in both man and society far more radical than any assumed or even desired by the mere reformists, who might be almost as horrified as Mr. Churchill himself at the radical newness of the new world which a more relentless pursuit of implications has led bolder thinkers to regard as inevitable.

Such bolder thinkers, far from accepting the contention that some belief, justified or illusory, in some degree of individual autonomy is a pragmatic necessity, would dismiss that contention as contemptuously as the present writer dismissed his example of "today's thinking." Man, they would say, is almost limitlessly plastic. He may be conditioned to almost anything—certainly to an acceptance of the belief that he is nothing but the product of his conditioning. In a world dominated by that conviction he would, they say, be as successful and as happy as his predecessor, conditioned to a belief in moral responsibility, would no doubt be unsuccessful and miserable.

Many who share the conviction of that Dean of the Humanities who announced "our approaching scientific ability to control men's thoughts with precision" are therefore not appalled by the prospect. Among them may be included B. F. Skinner, Professor of Psychology at Harvard, one of the most able and esteemed leaders in his field, and author of a fantasy called *Walden Two* which describes the contented life led by the inmates of an institution—though Professor Skinner might dislike this designation—to which they have voluntarily committed themselves and where they are conditioned to like being conditioned. An analysis of Professor Skinner's thought will reveal very clearly in what direction some believe that the Science of Man is moving.

Walden Two is a utopian community created by an experimental psychologist named Frazier who has learned the techniques for controlling thought with precision and who has conditioned his subjects to be happy, obedient and incapable of antisocial behavior. Universal benevolence and large tolerance of individual differences reign—not because it is assumed, as the founders of such utopias generally do assume, that they are natural to all innocent men uncorrupted by society—but because an experimental scientist, having at last mastered the "scientific ability to control men's thoughts with precision," has caused them to think benevolently and tolerantly.

An appeal to reason in contradistinction to passion, habit, or mere custom has been the usual basis of utopias from Plato to Sir Thomas More and even down to Samuel Butler. Mr. Skinner's is, on the other hand, distinctly modern in that it puts its faith in the conditioned reflex instead, and proposes to perfect mankind by making individual men incapable of anything except habit and prejudice. At Walden Two men behave in a fashion we are accustomed to call "reasonable," not because they reason, but because they do not; because "right responses" are automatic. At the very beginning of the story we are shown a flock of sheep confined to the area reserved for them by a single thread which long ago replaced the electric fence once employed to condition them not to wander. As predicted in official Communist theory, the State—represented here by electricity—has "withered away" and no actual restraint is necessary to control creatures in whom obedience has become automatic. Obviously the assumption is that what will work with sheep will work with men.

Now though men can reason, they are not exclusively reasoning creatures. None, therefore, of the classic utopias could be realized because each is based on the assumption that reason alone can be made to guide human behavior. Moreover—and what is perhaps more important—few people have ever seriously wished to be exclusively rational.

The good life which most desire is a life warmed by passions and touched with that ceremonial grace which is impossible without some affectionate loyalty to traditional forms and ceremonies. Many have, nevertheless, been very willing to grant that a little more reason in the conduct of private and public affairs would not be amiss. That is why, as fantasies, the utopias of Plato and Sir Thomas More have seemed interesting, instructive, even inspiring. But who really wants, even in fancy, to be, as Walden Two would make him, more unthinking, more nearly automatic than he now is? Who, even in his imagination, would like to live in a community where, instead of thinking part of the time, one never found it possible to think at all?

Is it not meaningful to say that whereas Plato's Republic and More's Utopia are noble absurdities, Walden Two is an ignoble one; that the first two ask men to be more than human, while the second urges them to be less? When, in the present world, men behave well, that is no doubt sometimes because they are creatures of habit as well as, sometimes, because they are reasonable. But if one proposes to change Man as Professor Skinner and so many other cheerful mechanists propose, is it really so evident that he should be changed in the direction they advocate? Is he something which, in Nietzsche's phrase, "must be surpassed," or is he a creature to whom the best advice one can give is the advice to retreat—away from such reasoned behavior as he may be capable of and toward that automatism of which he is also capable.

Obviously Walden Two represents—glorified, perfected,

THE MEASURE OF MAN

and curiously modernized—that ideal of a "cloistered virtue" which European man has tended to find not only
unsatisfactory as an ideal but almost meaningless in terms
of his doubtless conflicting aspirations. Nevertheless it
must be admitted that Thomas Henry Huxley, a proto-
modern, once admitted in an often quoted passage that
"if some great power would agree to make me always
think what is true and do what is right, on condition of
being turned into a sort of clock and wound up every
morning before I got out of bed, I should instantly close
with the offer." And what a Huxley would have agreed
to, prospective candidates for admission into Walden Two
might also find acceptable.

Frazier himself is compelled to make a significant confession: the motives which led him to undertake his successful experiment included a certain desire to exercise
power over his fellows. That is not admirable in itself
and is obviously not without its dangers. But he insists
that the danger will disappear with him because those
who succeed to his authority and inherit his techniques
will have enjoyed, as he did not, the advantages of a scientific conditioning process and that therefore such potentially antisocial impulses as his will no longer exist. In
other words, though the benevolent dictator is a rare phenomenon today, the happy chance which produced this
one will not have to be relied on in the future. Walden
Two will automatically produce the dictators necessary to
carry it on.

Nevertheless and even if the skeptical reader will grant for the sake of argument that automatic virtue represents an ideal completely satisfactory, a multitude of other doubts and fears are likely to arise in his mind. He will remember of course that Brook Farm and the rest failed promptly and decisively. Perhaps he will remember also that Russian communism achieved at least some degree of permanence only by rejecting, more and more completely, everything which in any way parallels the mildness, the gentleness, and the avoidance of all direct restraints and pressures which is characteristic of Walden Two; that the makers of Soviet policy came to denounce and repress even that somewhat paradoxical enthusiasm for the culture of a different world which was as much encouraged in the earliest days of the experiment as it is at Walden Two.

Hence, if a Walden Two is possible it obviously has become so only because—and this is a point which presumably Mr. Skinner himself wishes to emphasize—it differs in several respects from all superficially similar projects. Like the Russian experiment it assumes that, for all practical purposes, man is merely the product of society; but it also assumes a situation which did not exist when the Communist state was set up: namely one in which "the scientific ability to control men's thoughts with precision" has fully matured.

Thus if the man upon whom the experiment is performed is nothing but the limitlessly plastic product of external processes operating upon him and is, by definition, incapable of any significant autonomous activity, he is also, in this case, a creature who has fallen into the hands of an ideally competent dictator. His desires, tastes, convictions and ideals are precisely what the experimenter wants to make them. He is the repository of no potentialities which can ever develop except as they are called forth by circumstances over which he has no control. Finally, of course, his happy condition is the result of the fortunate accident which determined that the "engineer" who created him and, indirectly, will create all of his progeny, was an experimenter whose own random conditioning happened to produce, not the monster who might just as likely have been the first to seize the power that science offered, but a genuinely benevolent dictator instead.

À propos this last premise it might, in passing, be remarked as a curious fact that though scientific method abhors the accidental, the uncontrollable and the unpredicted; though Mr. Skinner's own ideal seems to be to remove forever any possible future intrusion of it into human affairs; yet the successful establishment of the first utopia depended ultimately on the decisive effect of just such an accident as will henceforth be impossible.

Critics of the assumption that technological advance is the true key to human progress have often urged that new powers are dangerous rather than beneficial unless the question of how they should be used is at least opened before the powers become available. With more than usual anxiety they might contemplate the situation in which we are now placed if it is true that only chance will answer the question by whom and in the interest of what "our approaching scientific ability to control men's thoughts with precision" is to be used. But this is only one of several desperate questions which the premises of *Walden Two* provoke. Most of them can also be related to points made by Mr. Skinner in less fanciful contexts and to one or two of them we may turn in connection with a more general consideration of problems raised if we are ready to assume that we actually do stand at the threshold of a world in which men's thoughts will be controlled scientifically and as a matter of course.

To begin with, we must, of course, abandon the old platitude, "You can't change human nature," and accept its opposite, "You can change human nature as much and in whatever direction you wish"—because "human nature" does not exist in the sense which the phrase implies. Whatever desires, tastes, preferences, and tendencies have been so general and so persistent as to create the assumption that they are innate or "natural" must be, as a matter of fact, merely the most ancient and deeply graven of the conditionings to which the human animal has been subjected. As Pascal—an odd thinker to be invoked in defense of a mechanistic and completely relativist ethic—once exclaimed in one of those terrifying speculations of which, no doubt, his own conditioning made him capable: "They say that habit is Second Nature; but perhaps Nature is only First Habit."

By eager reformers "You can't change human nature"

63

has often been denounced as both a counsel of despair and a convenient excuse for lazy indifference in the face of the world's ills. Yet the fact or alleged fact which the phrase attempts to state has also its positive aspect. To say that human nature cannot be changed means that human nature is something in itself and there is at least the possibility that part of this something is valuable. If we say that it cannot be changed we are also saying that it cannot be completely corrupted; that it cannot be transformed into something which we would not recognize as human at all. This is what the eighteenth century allowed Pope to say for it, and as long as one holds the doctrine that the term Nature actually describes some enduring set of possibilities and values, then some limit is set, not only to human perfectibility, but also, and more encouragingly, to things which it can become or be made.

But once this view of "Nature" has been dismissed as an illusion and even what appear to be the most persistent of its traits are thought of as merely the result of conditioning, then there is no limit to the extent to which men may become different from what they now are. There is nothing against which it may be assumed that human nature will revolt. Only by a temporarily established convention is any kind of vice a "creature of so frightful mien." Anything can be made to seem "natural." Cruelty, treachery, slander and deceit might come generally to seem not frightful but beautiful. And if it be said that the successful putting into practice of certain recent political philosophies supports the contention of determinists that man may, indeed, be taught to believe precisely this, it must be added that something more is also implied: namely that we must abandon—along with the conviction that human nature cannot be changed—all the hopes expressed in such phrases as "human nature will in the end revolt against" this or that.

Since no human nature capable of revolting against anything is now presumed to exist, then some other experimenter—conditioned perhaps as the son of the commandant of a Nazi labor camp—might decide to develop a race of men who found nothing more delightful than the infliction of suffering, and to establish for them a colony to be called Walden Three. By what standards could the dictator of Walden Two presume to judge that his utopia was any more desirable than its new rival? He could not appeal to God's revealed word; to the inner light of conscience; or to that eighteenth-century stand-by, the voice of Nature. He could say only that the accidents of his previous existence in a world where accident still played its part in determining how an individual should be conditioned had conditioned him to prefer what he would, in full realization of the unjustifiability of the metaphor, call "light rather than darkness." The life in Walden Two appears to him as "good" but the adjective would, of course, have no meaning in relation to anything outside himself.

In the light of such possibilities those who have not yet been molded by either Walden Two or Walden Three will tend to feel that before the "scientific ability to control men's thoughts with precision" has been fully utilized

c

by whoever may seize the limitless power it will confer, we had better take a last look around—if not for that way of escape which may not exist, then at least in order to grasp certain implications and possible consequences as they appear to the minds of men who are still "free"—free at least in the limited sense that they are the product of conditions which were brought about, in part, through the presence of random factors destined to play a smaller and smaller part in determining human personality. That second generation of dictators to whom the dictator of Walden Two expects to pass on the control of affairs will be conditioners who have themselves been conditioned. The circle of cause and effect will have been closed and no man will ever again be anything which his predecessor has not consciously willed him to be.

According to the mechanist's own theories, everything which happened in the universe from its beginning down, at least until yesterday, was the result of chance. The chemical molecule didn't "want" or "plan" to grow more complex until it was a protein; the protein did not plan to become protoplasm; and the amoeba did not plan to become man. As a matter of fact, a theory very popular at the moment explains the fact that life seems to have arisen on our earth but once in all the billions of years of the planet's existence by saying that it could arise only as the result of a combination of circumstances so fantastically improbable that they have never occurred again. Yet though they owe to chance both their very existence and all progress from the protozoan to civilization, they

are eager to take a step which would make it forever impossible for the unexpected and the unplanned to erupt
again into the scheme which will pass completely under
their own control.

No doubt many practical-minded people will object that
such speculations as these are a waste of time. After all,
they will say, even Walden Two does not exist except in
fancy and no one has yet claimed that the "approaching
scientific ability to control men's thoughts with precision"
has already arrived. Logical dilemmas and metaphysical
difficulties are cobwebs which will not entangle those who
refuse to take seriously their gossamer threads. We have
work to do and practical problems to solve.

But to all such it may be replied that practical problems
and the metaphysical forms to which they may be reduced
are not so unrelated as they may think, and that the logical extreme sometimes serves to make clear the real nature
of a purely practical problem. It is true that no man has
yet established a Walden Two or Walden Three, and that
neither has any man yet controlled *with precision* men's
thoughts. But it is also true that there has been a movement in a direction which suggests Walden Two as an
ideal. Moreover, statesmen, educators and publicists have
already achieved considerable success in their frankly admitted attempts to use the techniques already developed
to control and condition large sections of the public and
have increasingly declared their faith in the desirability
and practicality of such methods in contradistinction to
what used to be called education, on the one hand, and

appeals to the enlightened understanding of the public, on the other. Already it has quite seriously and without any conviction of cynicism been proposed that the advertisers' principle, "say a thing often enough and it will be believed," be utilized by those who have what they regard as "correct" or "healthy" or "socially useful" ideas to sell. Every time it is proposed that schools should develop certain attitudes in their pupils or that the government should undertake propaganda along a certain line, the question of the difficult distinction between education in some old-fashioned sense and "conditioning" definitely arises.

Moreover, it is because the techniques of the social scientist and the experimental psychologists do to some extent work that some attempt must be made to understand their implications. By their methods many men may be made to do and think many things. Already in the relatively simple case of education versus "useful conditioning," the difficult distinction ceases to be difficult once a border line has been definitely crossed. Writing to George Washington not long after our particular democracy had been founded, Thomas Jefferson remarked, "It is an axiom in my mind that our liberty can never be safe but in the hands of the people themselves, and that, too, of the people with a certain degree of instruction." What would Jefferson have thought of the suggestion that "a certain degree of instruction" be interpreted to mean "a certain degree of conditioning"? Would he not have pointed out that the distinction between the two is clear and fundamental; that "conditioning" is achieved by methods which by-pass or, as it were, short-circuit those very reasoning faculties which education proposes to cultivate and exercise? And would he not have added that democracy can have no meaning or no function unless it is assumed that these faculties do lie within a realm of freedom where the sanctions of democracy arise?

Thus the whole future of mankind may well depend not only on the question whether man is entirely or only in part the product of conditionings, but also on the extent to which he is treated as though he were. Will we come ultimately to base what we call "education," in and out of schools, on the assumption that conditioning by propaganda as well as other methods is the most effective, even if it is not the only, method of influencing human beings.

To all such questions an answer in pragmatic terms has already been given at least positively enough to make it very pertinent to ask into whose hands the power already being exercised is to fall; to ask who is to decide in what direction the citizen is to be conditioned, and on the bases of what standards of value those decisions are to be made. That is simply the practical aspect of the theoretical question, "Who shall be master of Walden Two?"

In the totalitarian countries, where deterministic theories have been accepted in their most unqualified form and the techniques of control most systematically practiced, the question just posed has been answered in the simplest possible manner, and very much in the same way that it was answered at Walden Two. Power is exercised by those who seized it and, theoretically at least, this seizure was the last event which could "happen" because henceforward human destiny will be in the hands of those who are now in a position to control it. The question whether they ought to have done so and whether it is well for humanity that they did was either always meaningless or soon to become so since all the value judgments made in the future will be made by those who have been conditioned to approve what has happened to them.

One result of all this is that during the transition period while there are still survivors from the age when men's minds had not yet been controlled with precision and a conflict of wills is still possible—*i.e.,* under the conditions prevailing in the totalitarian states as they actually exist— a sharp distinction has to be made between those in possession of the power which they have seized and those who are subject to their manipulations. As a catchword the old term "classless society" may be used, but it is evident that no two classes could be more widely separated than the class of those who decide what shall be done and the class of those who are conditioned and controlled.

Obviously such a situation cannot arise either in Germany, Russia or Walden Two until the seizure of power has actually occurred and the power seized must include not only the classic essential, "the instruments of production," but also those "instruments of thought control" which seem to be assuming a more crucial importance than Marx assigned them.

No less obviously this seizure has not yet been made in the countries still called "democratic." Power may be drifting into the hands of certain groups but most of the members of these groups are not quite so completely committed as the totalitarian leaders were to the theories by which they justified their acts and are therefore not so ready to assume the dictatorship which may possibly be already within their reach. In such countries it is, therefore, still possible to consider certain questions, both practical and metaphysical, which even those still capable of considering them are forbidden to raise publicly in totalitarian states. We can still think—or at least go through those mental motions which were formerly called thinking—about the direction in which our own society seems to be moving, about certain large questions of values and ethics, even about the possibilities that under certain conditions men may not be the automata they are more and more assumed to be and that therefore their thoughts never can be controlled either completely or "with precision." Even more specifically we may ask whether totalitarianism on either the model of Soviet Russia or Walden Two is what we wish for or must inevitably accept.

It has sometimes been said that the totalitarian state is merely what democracy must in time become. Enthusiastically in the one case, reluctantly in the other, the same premises lead to the same methods and the same methods to the same results. What one proclaims definitively as dogma is the same as what the other drifts toward and this distinction is the only one which can be made, no matter where we attempt to draw it. In this view a "people's democracy" is only a "welfare state" which has fully accepted its implications. In theory as well as in practice the difference is always merely in the degree to which the logic of any position has been followed to its ultimate conclusion.

No doubt reality is much less simple. But after this large proviso has been accepted much can be said to support the contention that what we of the democracies toy with and lean toward are the same scientific hypotheses and the same philosophical notions that totalitarians proclaim as truths it is forbidden to question.

Roman Catholic doctrine makes the useful distinction between those beliefs which are *de fide* and those which are no more than *pia sententia.* The one must be accepted without dispute by all who wish to remain within the fold; the other, though part of commonly held opinion, have the weight of no authority behind them. In many cases the distinction between what the Communist state proclaims concerning the real nature of man and the proper methods of dealing with it differs from what many of our own psychologists and sociologists tend to assume only as an article of belief which has been proclaimed *de fide* differs from *pia sententia.* What we may tend to deduce from, say, the Pavlovian experiments does not differ too significantly from what an orthodox Russian scientist would say that these same experiments have proved with ultimate finality.

In what the sociologist previously quoted was pleased to call "today's thinking" man tends to appear very much what the Russian version of Marxist science would make him and those who follow such lines of thought are inevitably led to the same next step. If man is the product of the conditioning to which chance has subjected him, why should we not make him what we would like him to be?

We have, it is said, already effectively asserted our control over nature, animate and inanimate. Technology has already entered its mature phase and biology is entering it. We have mastered the atom; we have also learned how both to breed and to train animals. Since man is part of nature he also should be subject to control and no more should be necessary to make him so than easy extensions of the methods already successfully applied. We boast that we have mastered nature but that mastery can hardly be called complete until human nature is at least as completely under our control as the other phenomena of animate nature have become.

Perhaps the most general aspect of this subtle but inclusive shift of emphasis is revealed in the almost unconscious substitution of one term for another when the characteristics of a good social order are discussed. At the beginning of the democratic movement the watchword was "opportunity." Social and political evils were thought of as impediments to the free development of aspirations and abilities. But because "opportunity" as an ideal implies faith in the autonomous powers of the individual it

C*

73

has given way to others embodied in words which suggest in one way or another, not what men may be permitted to do for themselves, but what with benevolent intentions of course may be done to them.

The most brutally frank of such words is of course "control" but it is used most freely by those who have come frankly to accept a barely disguised totalitarian ideal. In those who wish still to pay lip service at least to some sort of faith in democracy and freedom the preferred words are "education," "adjustment" and, with a closer approach to frankness, "conditioning." But the difference is one of degree, not in the fundamental assumption which is that men should not be left to develop but must have their characters and temperaments, as well as their daily lives, somehow "planned" for them. The most benign aspect of this assumption is revealed in the desire for a "welfare state" which will assure the physical well-being of its citizens. The most sinister aspect is that more fully revealed in the speculations of the most advanced and theoretical social psychologists who have passed on, as the author of *Walden Two* has, to consider how the character, opinions and tastes of the individual may also be "planned" for him.

No doubt many of those who agree with that Dean of the Humanities to whose happy phrase we find ourselves again and again recurring would speak with the customary horror of the frankly totalitarian states which have, to date, achieved the greatest success in controlling men's thoughts with precision. They would carefully avoid such frank terms as "brain washing" which the Communists use to state clearly their intentions. But it is difficult to see what difference there is except the difference between a philosophy which is still tentative and somewhat reluctant to admit its ultimate implications and one which, facing those implications, proceeds confidently to put into practice the techniques which it has found effective. If "adjustment" is not to become "control" and "conditioning" is to stop short of "brain washing," some limits must be set which are not defined or even hinted at in such statements as those made by some psychologists.

Even those of us whose convictions permit us to doubt that men's thoughts will ever be completely controlled with absolute "precision" must realize, nevertheless, that the "scientific ability" to control them to some considerable degree has been growing and that in all probability it will grow still further. The terrifying extent to which many (if not all) the individuals in a group may be made to act and think in ways which we would once have thought inconceivable is already all too evident. Hence the question of how that power, whether it be limited or unlimited, will be used in our own society is of immediate as well as remote importance. It is no longer merely a metaphysical one.

It does no good to say that the democracy to which we assure ourselves we are committed safeguards us against the arbitrary use of that power. To say anything of the sort is merely to beg the question because an essential part of the question has to do with the reasonable doubt whether what we call democracy can survive the maturing techniques for determining in advance what "the voice of the people" will say. "Democracy," as the West defined it and in contradistinction to the new definition which totalitarianism has attempted to formulate, is meaningless except on the assumption that the individual man's thoughts and desires are to some extent uncontrollable and unpredictable. There can be no possible reason for taking a vote if the results can either be determined or even predicted in advance. In a society which assures, rightly or wrongly, that events are predictably determined, elections can be no more than those rituals with only a formal, ceremonial significance which, in Soviet Russia and Nazi Germany, they actually became.

In Walden Two this fact is tacitly recognized. Its founding dictator expects authority to "wither away" at the time of his death if not before, precisely as, in Communist theory, the dictatorship of the party will some day wither. But before withering away has occurred, the whole future history of mankind will have been set in a pattern which can never suffer any fundamental change because it must correspond to the pattern of conditionings which are self-perpetuating once they have been firmly and universally established. It is hard to see how we can accept even pragmatically the convictions and ideals of Walden Two without incurring consequences which correspond in the realm of the actual to the theoretical consequences of its theoretical premises. The question whether our own society is in the process of turning itself into some sort of Walden Two is far from being merely fantastic.

4

THE IDOLS OF THE LABORATORY

O F COURSE "it" has not actually happened here. The convictions toward which we may seem to have been drifting and the techniques with which we have certainly been experimenting have not yet created the kind of society which these convictions, backed up by these techniques, may be capable of producing.

The most that can be said is what we have already said: namely that the means and methods we have developed are leading us on to other methods and ends which many neither criticize nor even recognize. We are drifting with a current of half-formulated preferences and judgments which conduct us we know not whither and sometimes in directions we might not want to take if we knew what the direction was.

Consider, for example, a simple situation somewhat different from that with which we have been concerned. Few of us would be willing to say that material goods are the only real goods and that increase in wealth and comfort is the only end worth pursuing. But just because we have learned effective methods of increasing both, we practice those methods with so much enthusiasm that we begin to act as though what they get us were the only things worth getting. And because we have not clearly formulated the other possible ends which we may vaguely acknowledge as desirable, we have carelessly accepted a materialistic philosophy which makes any definition of these other ends difficult. Thus we act as though we believed what many of us would not confess to believing. In the very early days of the Second World War a popular writer on economic subjects warned us not to forget when we came to choose sides that contemporary Germany represented the highest stage which civilization had yet reached. And the proof offered was this: under Hitler production per man hour had reached a level never previously achieved!

Only by a criticism of the *ends* for which new powers may be used can the threat which they carry be minimized. And by "criticism" is meant not only that sort of public discussion which a given political situation may or may not permit, but also a genuine consideration of ends as well as means, a reopening of the question of what we want as possibly opposed to what it has now become possible to get: in a word, a renewed examination of our *value judgments*.

Yet criticism of this sort has now become extremely difficult if we attempt to apply it to the whole subject of

78

the general intentions of those who claim to be acquiring a new power over men's thoughts. Such criticism inevitably becomes metaphysical, and the thesis of the positivists is that the metaphysical is essentially meaningless, or at least ineffectual. Even the general public which could not state its convictions so rigorously is at least committed to the belief that metaphysics is moonshine and that only "practical" matters are worth discussing. Yet we are finally thrown back upon the metaphysical question whether legitimate value judgments really are possible and whether, if they are not, dispensing with them necessarily opens the way to possibilities which seem to many of us no less revolting than they are disastrous.

Even the most moderate proponents of a "scientific" morality seem usually unaware of the closed circle around which they lead us when they consent to consider questions concerning value. They begin by saying—and it seems reasonable enough—that value judgments should be based on knowledge rather than on tradition or intuition; and they bid us, before we make them, to consult not merely the physical sciences but also such other bodies of available knowledge as history and anthropology. Unfortunately, however, it has usually turned out that when they follow their own advice the conclusion which they arrive at is not that a true value judgment has been scientifically justified but that the impossibility of making such a judgment has been demonstrated.

As far back as the nineteenth century this pattern was set by Lecky's great *History of European Morals* which undertook to study scientifically the ethical systems which had actually prevailed. The conclusion reached was summed up in Lecky's famous statement that there is no possible line of conduct which has not, at some time and place, been condemned, and which has not, at some other time and place, been enjoined as a duty. Thus what he arrived at was not a "scientific morality" but only the conviction that such a scientific morality is impossible; that, at least from the standpoint of science, "morals" are indistinguishable from "manners" or "mores" and that "the good" is nothing more than "the prevalent."

Anthropology—which is only history with an extended scope—has more recently been more fashionable as a body of knowledge to which the moralist may appeal. But one of the most prevalent, or at least the most popular, schools of anthropology has been that which defends a cultural relativism corresponding quite closely to the moral relativism of Lecky. In the United States Ruth Benedict's *Patterns of Culture* has probably been the most widely read of all anthropological works, and *Patterns of Culture* is devoted to the thesis that the scientist must concern himself, not with any attempt to define the characteristics of a *good* society, but only with the attempt to get an adequate understanding of the fact that the "patterns of culture" which have actually existed are almost infinitely varied and that any one of them may be "good" from the standpoint of those who live in accordance with it. Thus the final conclusion seems to be, not that anthropology can tell us objectively what a good society is, but rather that the question, when considered objectively, has no meaning.

It is true that Miss Benedict falls into the inconsistency to which all who deny that they are making value judgments usually fall. She is objective enough when she compares, say, the "Apollonian" culture of the Hopis with the "Dionysian" culture of some of the Plains Indians. But when she turns, as she does, to describe the Babbitt or Middletown culture—which she takes to be predominant in the United States at the moment of writing—nearly everything she says is loaded with an adverse judgment of that culture.

To be consistent she should say that Rotary Clubs and the ceremonies of the businessman's golf game cannot be objectively pronounced either good or bad since they are, like the Hopi snake dance, simply part of a pattern of culture. What actually happens is, of course, that her objectivity deserts her just as soon as she considers the culture of her own tribe and that she makes value judgments on it just as freely—but with much less awareness of what she is doing—as they are made by those ignorant of the science of anthropology but loyal to tradition, metaphysics, or intuition.

Moreover, and in so far as those who advocate a "scientific" morality actually do consistently follow the conclusions to which they are led, the practical result is to encourage the tendency, already strongly developed in our society, to make no distinction between what men do and what they "ought" to do; to turn the quest for scientific morality into nothing except a study of prevalent behavior.

To state that "whatever is is right" and to accept that statement fully or absolutely requires a metaphysical analysis of which most men are not capable and leads to conclusions which most men would probably hesitate to accept. But many if not most men are now pragmatically accepting it already when they propose to use studies of everything from the reading habits of adolescence to the sexual behavior of homosexuals as the bases for ordering the educational system or setting up standards of sexual morality. Thus though the assumption that the concept represented in the word "ought" is radically meaningless is one not usually consciously made it is nevertheless the assumption on which many "advanced thinkers" seem willing to proceed.

Hence it appears that when the advocates of the theory that value judgments should be based on knowledge actually follow consistently their principles, they end by admitting that the only thing which science can achieve is the discovery of what the most usual conduct is like. The only guidance they can offer is the suggestion that we should not expect anything other than what we find to be happening and this in turn comes down to little more than the statement "what has been has been, what will be will be."

No sociological determinist thoughtful enough to realize the implications of his position fails to recognize that questions concerning value must be answered some-how and he usually answers them by saying that though no value judgments arrived at by metaphysical processes are valid, there is something which serves the purpose which the so-called value judgments cannot really serve and takes their place in any functioning society. This something is provided for us by the contingencies of the natural world and, in the long run, would prevent the sustained development or continued existence of such per-verse horrors as Nazism achieved or imagination may fear in a Walden Three.

Since Professor Skinner is one of the clearest and most persuasive exponents of this position we may again use him for the purpose of criticizing his statement of it both as implied in *Walden Two* and as explicitly defended elsewhere. Essentially his position is defined by the state-ment that there are certain "values" which are "self-evi-dent" and that no human choice is necessarily involved in the acceptance of them. We do not "make" value judg-ments but they are imposed upon us.

And yet, as we shall see, this thesis breaks down as it always does when confronted by the fact that these "self-evident values" are not recognized as self-evident by every-one and therefore can be called self-evident only with the proviso that those to whom they do not seem so are de-clared to be not "normal" or "sane"—by the arbitrary standard set up by individuals who insist that they are not setting any arbitrary standards.

Anyone who believes in the all but unlimited effect of

83

the conditioning to which every mind has been subjected ought logically to be the first to suspect that when a man calls something "self-evident" that means merely that he has been early and firmly conditioned to believe it; not at all that it would appear self-evident to those who happen to have been otherwise conditioned. Thus those who follow Mr. Skinner's line of argument may be hoisted very neatly on their own petards. While they profess to make no value judgment they are actually making one in the most absolute and unconditional way possible, namely, by saying "it is obviously true." And whatever dangers may be involved in accepting as absolutely true conclusions arrived at by the fallible processes of human reason it does not seem as though they could be avoided by refusing to think at all—which appears to be what Mr. Skinner is proposing when faced with an ultimate problem.

In his case the value judgment which he makes while insisting that it is not really a value judgment at all comes down to this: Whatever contributes to the health of an individual or the long-continued survival of the society of which he is a part is "good," or, as he put it in the course of a debate, "The one criterion that is thrust upon us is whether the group which observes a given practice will be here tomorrow." The implication is that, granted this premise, we can easily determine how a society should be planned and to what opinions, tastes, and activities an individual should be conditioned.

But what this, in its turn, really comes down to is, of course, only a rather fancy restatement of the doctrine implied in the phrase "survival of the fittest." And the semantic emptiness of the doctrine was long ago exposed by asking the simple question, "Fittest for what?" The only possible answer is "fittest to survive" which closes the circle and thereby reduces the statement to complete nonsense by making it read: "Those survive who survive."

For the moment the question is not whether the value judgment which declares "survival" and "health" to be goods is defensible either as one of those arbitrary choices which some declare all value judgments to be or as something at which reason can arrive. The question is simply whether or not they are "self-evident" goods in the sense that all men not certifiably insane have accepted them and that they therefore demonstrate how easily we may escape the necessity of making, for ourselves, any value judgments at all.

It is certainly not self-evident or universally admitted that if, as some believe, the intellectual acuteness and artistic genius of the ancient Athenians cut short the life of their state, then this acuteness and this genius were so far from being good that it would have been better if Greek thought and Greek art had never existed. Neither is it self-evident that the Egyptian civilization of the first and second dynasties—which historians have called the most enduring societies ever known—was also the most admirable and "right." May we not say instead that long survival is no more self-evidently the final measure of the worth of a society than it is of an individual and that by

85

no means everyone agrees that the longest-lived men are
the best, or that he who lives dully and viciously to the
age of one hundred has demonstrated that his life was
better than that of a man who dies at fifty after a full·and
fruitful career—or even, for that matter, after a short but
merry one. Miss Edna Millay, as is well known, advised
burning the candle at both ends, and though she may very
well have been misguided, she was certainly not insane.
Mr. Skinner's self-evident values were not self-evident to
her.

One does not—to carry the argument a little further—
need to accept Christian ethics to remember that the foun-
der of Christianity is reported to have been so far from
believing that "survival value" provided an ultimate test
of the good that he said on one occasion, "He who loses
his life shall gain it."

More than one biologist has remarked that the cockroach seems to be one of the most successful as well as
one of the most stable of living organisms. Only a trained
entomologist can distinguish any difference between those
species living today and their fossilized ancestors who
flourished some 250 million years ago. Throughout all
these millennia their philosophy has worked. To Mr. Skinner's test question, "Will it be here tomorrow?" the members of the cockroach society can reply "Yes" with more
justifiable confidence than could the members of any human society. Are we really forced to the conclusion that
the cockroach's success is the only sort which can have
any meaning? Are there no reasons why it is "better" to

be a man than an insect? If there are, then some criterion other than the promise of continued survival must be applicable. For insects, for individuals, and for societies alike, there are ignoble as well as noble ways of surviving.

Once criticism of Mr. Skinner's first principles has been insisted on, it becomes obvious enough that "survival" and "health" are not actually ends at all but only means. Unless one survives *for* something, neither survival nor health has any value in itself. But the answer to the question what things are worth living for is not self-evident and thus the attempt to avoid value judgments leads back around the same circle to which every attempt to make a science do something of which it is incapable inevitably leads.

If we permit ourselves to develop methods or means which lead only to other methods and other means, not to any humanly valuable end, then both individual men and society must either live for the sake of their techniques—much as misers live for their money rather than for anything which it can buy—or they will pursue ends unacknowledged and unrecognized. Either the "self-evident" truths become a set of dogmas ferociously defended from criticism or we drift with a current of half-formulated preferences and judgments which conduct us we know not whither and sometimes in a direction contrary to that in which we would like to go.

In the totalitarian states the first of these possibilities has been more or less completely realized. In our own

87

society—still protected by those "inner contradictions" which so distress the fanatical—we have not, so far at least, paid the full penalty for philosophizing badly. Perhaps that is partly because we have not fully accepted either the philosophy or the practice of totalitarianism and hence permit older ideals to temper somewhat the new. Perhaps it is also because the impossibility of not philosophizing at all manifests itself slowly and we have not yet reached the point of acquiescing in exclusive dogmas without knowing that we acquiesce in any dogmas at all.

What happens—and what is actually happening—is, that when critical awareness fades away, remoter and remoter deductions are made from the unexamined premises until conclusions are reached which even those who accept the premises might reject if they could follow the chain of unconscious and dubious logic by which they were led to them.

Take for example this matter of "health." Even before the meaning of the word is extended by metaphorical use to include the less easily definable "mental health" the value set on what the term implies soon goes beyond anything which could possibly be called self-evident. Not merely does "health" come to mean the absence of disease and a satisfactory physical fitness, but it begins to exalt a more and more perfect health and a more and more complete "fitness," regardless of the fact that health, like cleanliness, is not susceptible of an indefinitely useful increase. The ultimate absurdity is reached in those clubs of young men who spend the day displaying their tanned skins and muscles on the California beaches where this "fitness" has become an acknowledged "end in itself." One cannot ask "health for what?" or "fit for what?" without introducing value judgments which are not self-evident and which the tribe of logical positivists warns us against. We cannot even ask what a healthy race should do with itself unless we are willing to philosophize, and without philosophizing we must end content with a fitness which does not seem to be actually fit for anything.

"In what does *mental* health consist?" and "To what extent ought 'mental health' be valued above any other mental characteristic?" are questions to which it is even more obvious that no answer can be given by those who refuse to philosophize—unless indeed one is willing to take it as self-evident that a troubled Mozart who died at thirty-five or even a Shakespeare who died at fifty-two is to be counted a man less successful than those who lived longer and whose minds were more obviously "healthy" than the minds which produced the G Minor quintet and *King Lear*—neither of which is likely to be counted, in the most obvious meaning of the word, self-evidently "healthy." Nor will it do to object that to call "health" self-evidently good means only "other things being equal." Things never can be equal if we start with the premise about "health" without examining or criticizing the assumed meaning of the word.

Many who are little disposed to either masochism or even ascetic practices have nevertheless found it meaningful as well as convenient to recognize what they call "divine discontent," and there are those who see in some sort of "soul sickness" the indispensable condition of a fully developed humanity. How is it possible, without some kind of philosophizing, to accept or reject what such terms imply? Is it really self-evident at what point "aspiration" (which is admirable) becomes merely "maladjustment" (which is not); or that a man's reach should never exceed his grasp? What of the old problem of the pig who is contented and the Socrates who is not?

Such terms as "normality" and "satisfactory adjustment" have, of course, to be defined by somebody. The statistician can determine the meaning of the first, if it is assumed to means "most usual." But the second will have to depend to some extent on the subjective preferences of some group. Fortunately, for them, that group is largely self-selecting in a society actively engaged in the attempt to mold the minds and characters of its members because the relatively aggressive, extraverted people are those who are temperamentally most likely to practice enthusiastically the available techniques for "conditioning." Thus it comes about that they are the ones who, in accord with their natures, provide the accepted definition.

Thus without the establishment of any totalitarian state or even the setting up of any Walden Two, merely by the rejection of all value judgments except those which a particular type of mind declares to be self-evident, we begin to evolve a mental climate with definitely recognizable characteristics. First it is "self-evident" that men ought to be healthy; then self-evident that "healthy" means "adjusted"; and then, finally, self-evident that "adjusted" means extraverted. "Doing" is therefore important and "thinking" can mean only "plans for doing" if it is to means anything at all and to question any of the accepted values is to demonstrate "maladjustment" or "immaturity."

In "today's thinking" the two statements commonly made or implied come down to this: (1) Value judgments cannot validly be made by any metaphysical process. (2) Value judgments do not need to be made because they are entirely self-evident to every "normal" mind. But even if we accept the first of these statements the second is demonstrably false by simple historical evidence. Sane people have not in the past always made the same ones and neither for that matter do all sane people today. "Today's thinking" may have effectively put us into a dilemma but it has not, as it claims, then released us from it. If it has demonstrated that value judgments are never valid it has not demonstrated that we do not make them, arbitrarily and irrationally if not reasonably and defensibly. If we cannot think effectively on the subject, choices are still possible and for good or for ill we do make them.

As influence, power, and authority in our society pass, as they are passing, from philosophers and theologians into the hands of those who call themselves "human engineers" whether they happen to be functioning as lawmakers, publicists, teachers, psychologists, or even advertising managers, it is passing from those who were at least aware of what value judgments they were making to those who are not; passing into the hands of men who act on very inclusive and fateful judgments while believing that they are acting on self-evident principles immune to criticism. They do not know what they are making us into and refuse to permit us even to ask. Moreover, in so far as their attempt to "condition" the human beings on whom they practice their techniques are successful, they make it less and less probable that their fateful assumptions will ever be questioned.

From the situation in which they have placed us there seems no possible escape so long as we accept the premises which most thoughtful as well as most thoughtless men seem today inclined to accept. If man is only an animal and an animal is only some kind of machine, then both must be controlled by laws. The power of choice which we seem sometimes to exercise and the decisions which we seem sometimes to make must be illusory because the laws of cause and effect are inexorable. Once these assertions have been accepted as fact it becomes almost inevitable to agree that human nature and conduct will eventually become as predictable and as controllable as the other phenomena of the natural world now are. And since the controllers are themselves only the product of their own conditioning the control which they will exercise is itself already predetermined. There remains nothing which we can do except to close our eyes and to say, "Here we go—to become what and in what future we cannot even guess."

Even though we may think that we are moving in the direction of our desire, that desire was predetermined by the forces which conditioned us to want what we think we are wanting. Whether that will turn out to be something like Huxley's *Brave New World,* like Skinner's *Walden Two,* or something quite different from either, we cannot know. What we do know is only that what will be, will be.

And what rough beast, its hour come round at last,
Slouches towards Bethlehem to be born?

5

THE MINIMAL MAN

So FAR, our discussion of "today's thinking"
has turned pretty persistently around a few brief quotations from three or four of "today's thinkers"—each of
whom seems to assume that man is either "nothing but"
the product of external forces operating upon him or at
least so largely such that psychology, education, and government should disregard whatever autonomous powers
he may have.

Mr. Lukas of the Society for the Prevention of Crime
has told us that "all antisocial behavior [and presumably
all prosocial behavior as well] is considered to be the result of unique economic, sociological, and psychological
factors in each offender's past history." The Dean of the
Humanities at the Massachusetts Institute of Technology
has assumed that we shall soon be able "to control men's
thoughts with precision." Professor Skinner has joyfully
imagined a utopian future in which we shall all be happy
and "well adjusted" because the premises of Mr. Lukas

and the Dean have been made the basis of a successful technique for conditioning all men to act in a certain way and to think certain things.

Inevitably the question how "representative" these thinkers are will be raised, and inevitably some readers will object that "most" psychologists and sociologists do not go so far in this direction. Obviously it is impossible to prove what "most people" think and for our purpose it is not necessary. For the moment our purpose is to define certain ideas to which we will ultimately oppose others. And for the moment therefore our need is to define as sharply as possible the assumptions which we intend to repudiate. At least some distinguished persons do make them in the extreme form which the quotations illustrate.

To say this is not to say that these same assumptions are not sometimes repudiated by other contemporary thinkers or even that such repudiation is not usual among those who represent the best as opposed to the lagging thinkers of our time. Choosing almost at random from among books published within the last year one might cite Reinhold Niebuhr's *The Irony of American History* which includes an attack upon the whole school of sociological determinists; Eric Voegelin's *The New Science of Politics* which reaffirms the primary reality of absolute "values"; and Nicolai Hartmann's *The New Ways of Ontology*, written to defend a middle ground between an idealism which asserts that mind plays the only decisive role in the shaping of history and a materialism which sees the universe as affected by nothing except "things."

But up to the present, at least, only a very small public is so much as aware that the points of view represented by the books just cited have ever been defined. They certainly do not represent what most men would recognize as "today's thinking," which has, so far as the general public is aware, tended to assume more and more completely that man is largely if not absolutely determined, predictable, and controllable. Perhaps this tendency represents the thinking of yesterday rather than of today; but it is still very widely accepted by those who are molding our institutions.

If the results of this tendency seem disastrous to those who do not want to see civilization ultimately become a Walden Two, then they must ask themselves on what basis they may oppose it; to what extent they may legitimately question the supposedly proved premises on which it rests. They must ask to what extent Man may hope to make free choices; to be responsible for his own conduct; to make, rather than to have imposed upon him, value judgments.

Those of us who do insist on asking these questions will ask them in terms far more modest than were once commonly employed when it was customary to state categorically that we are all "the captains of our souls." We will not expect, hope, or perhaps even want, to believe about ourselves what men at other times took for granted. Responsibility as full and as absolute as has sometimes been assumed is a terrible burden as well as a privilege. The important roles played by the mechanisms of heredity, by forgotten psychic traumas, and by the conditioning factors in the social environment will be—and perhaps gladly—accepted, just as the effectiveness of the techniques developed for predicting and controlling the beliefs as well as the behavior of large masses of men will be acknowledged. We will not expect to be able again to exclaim "What a piece of work .is man; how infinite in capacity; in understanding how like a God," while believing that statement to be a full or complete account of the kind of creature Man is. Our protest will perhaps go no further than to ask whether the rival account offered by mechanistic social psychologists is itself as full and complete as we have been assured that it is.

Perhaps, indeed, before being so bold as to ask even that question, we will pose to ourselves another so purely hypothetical that those uninterested in merely hypothetical questions will not, for the moment, need even to attend: If men must now recognize that they are no more than machines, then at what point did they forfeit the right to talk about "Man" as though he were unique? What are the *minimal* powers and characteristics one would have to possess to be worthy of the designation Man? If these minimal specifications turn out to be modest enough, then perhaps we will be permitted the question we did not dare to ask before: Do these *minimum* specifications still include things which our real knowledge of the human animal positively forbids us to attribute to it?

D

The more closely we examine them the more modest the minimum specifications turn out to be. They certainly do not require us to affirm that the minimal man is completely autonomous, never predictable, and always beyond the reach of conditioning or manipulation. It is, we must remember, not we but the mechanists who deal in absolutes and are dogmatically inclined to "nothing but" generalizations. Their claims are not minimal but maximum. The forked stick in which they hold us will hold us only so long as their arguments admit of no qualifications and no exceptions.

If men are even sometimes and to some degree capable of independent choices, then men are not wholly or always the victims of their environment. And if those who deny that men are ever to that extent free go one step beyond what their evidence proves, they cannot logically compel us to accept their conclusions. If, for instance, they are ever guilty of using the negative argument which runs: "My methods enable me to prove that so and so often happens; my methods do not enable me to prove that the contrary ever does; therefore I assume that the 'often' means 'always,'" we can reply that the assumption is no more than an assumption and that if we have reasons for doubting that assumption our reasons may be given without our being to the slightest degree "unscientific." We shall, on the contrary, be more scientific than those who assert positively what they cannot prove.

These reasons, when we come to them, will not necessarily include any denial that "man is an animal" or even, perhaps, that he is "nothing but an animal." Our minimum specifications include only capacities in which the animal may also, to some lesser degree, have his share so that between us and him there need be no absolute discontinuity. The minimal beast—who is not quite a machine—could be a beast who has started on the road which leads ultimately to the minimal man and we still may be brothers because we both may be children of Nature rather than of God.

Grant us only that what we call "reasoning" is not always rationalization; that consciousness can sometimes be more than merely an epiphenomenon accompanying behavior; that "value judgments," even if never more than "tastes" or "preferences," are nevertheless not absolutely and "nothing but" what we have been conditioned to accept—grant us this and those minimal concessions will free us from the dilemma in which the refusal to make them has placed us. They are levers with which, once more, we can move our world. They may possibly make us again "good enough to survive"; they are even more likely to make survival seem worth having. Perhaps they may also relieve us of that burden of anxiety and guilt which the sense that we had surrendered our humanity imposed on us.

Instead of saying to himself, "I am the product of my environment and will be compelled both to believe and to do what my infantile conditioning and my social environment have predetermined," the Minimal Man would say to himself something like this: "I am both an individual and part of an aggregate. The behavior of that aggregate, as statistically measured, may be something to some large extent determined by forces outside any individual, because most individuals do not exercise even to the degree of which they are capable the minimal freedom which, for them also, could exist. To some extent I no doubt move with that aggregate, doing what it does, thinking what it thinks, and I am perhaps destined to meet the fate it meets. But there is also some area of possibility within which I can move as an independent particle. I have some scope for choice and action. I have my realm of freedom as well as my realm of contingency. Henceforward, I shall cultivate an awareness of that realm of freedom, refuse to deny its existence just because it has, in my time, been less investigated and emphasized than the realm of bondage. I shall do at least part of my thinking on the premise that such a realm exists for others as well as for me. I shall live part of my inner as well as part of my outer life where I am aware of the extent to which I am free rather than of the extent to which I am not.

"Who knows how large that area of freedom is; how influential the example I set may be; or within what limits the behavior of the aggregate itself may be changed if some considerable number of the atoms which compose it realize that atoms, even the atoms of dead matter, do not, as individuals, obey the statistical laws of determinism? I shall act as though I were at least a Minimal Man and perhaps I will discover that this Minimal Man is 'good enough to survive.' "

After he had completed his visit to Walden Two, the narrator in Mr. Skinner's fantasy summarized some of the conclusions to which he had been led. For society as a whole to achieve what had been accomplished there: "Education would have to abandon the technical limitations it had imposed upon itself and step forth into the broader sphere of human engineering. Nothing short of the complete revision of a culture would suffice."

The words chosen are gentle and reassuring; very much indeed like that other gentle term "re-education," which we have recently seen given in other lands a new and terrifying definition. But what can the gentle terms used by Mr. Skinner really mean? What does it mean for "education to abandon the technical limitations which it has imposed upon itself" if it does not mean that it shall stop concerning itself with those processes of education which put their faith in the effectiveness of the cultivated powers of reasoning and go in for "conditioning" instead? What can "going forth into the broader sphere of human engineering" mean if it does not mean undertaking to do with men what the experimental psychologist has learned how to do with rats? What does "the complete revision of a culture" imply if it does not imply, as it always has ended by implying: those who will not accept re-education will have to be liquidated?

Considerations like those which have occupied the past

THE MEASURE OF MAN

few pages cannot, of course, have any real meaning unless the Minimal Man really exists. If it has been conclusively demonstrated that all animals, including man, are merely machines, and that the behavior of a machine is fully determined; if what seems uncontrollable and unpredictable is only that which we have not yet learned enough about; then the assumption that some realm of freedom exists is an impossible assumption. Before we go any further with it we should examine a little more closely the proofs offered by those who assert that it is.

Have they or have they not proved as much as they sometimes say that they have? Do they themselves sometimes go beyond their own evidence? Are they guilty of claiming to have ruled out a possibility when they have actually done no more than say, "What we have been unable to measure or use by the methods we have chosen and for the purposes we have in mind, does not exist." Finally, and if their negative proofs turn out to be less than final, we should ask ourselves what positive reasons we ourselves may have for believing that what has not been proved impossible may in fact be both possible and actual.

The more absolute and unqualified the contentions of any mechanist happen to be, the more likely he is to insist that "science proves" them true. Let us consider for a moment, not the persuasiveness of his theories, but the extent to which they have actually been demonstrated.

How much of his creed do we have to accept simply because we cannot do otherwise?

To begin with, it is certainly not true that "today's thinking" is the inescapable result of what the laboratory has demonstrated. Merely to watch Pavlov's dogs or somebody else's rats would not, by itself, lead any sane man to say, "Obviously, free will is dead." The fact that the digestive juices begin to run in the canine stomach when the dinner bell rings does not, after all, demonstrate that all antisocial behavior is the result of individual conditioning! Neither, for that matter, is anything of the sort really demonstrated by the success of the advertiser in selling his wares or even the success—when he has it—of the sociologist in re-educating the delinquent youth.

By themselves such facts are perfectly compatible with the simultaneous existence of a realm of freedom. No one ever doubted that the Maximal, much less the Minimal, Man is sometimes and to some extent influenced by his circumstances. Even those who in the past have seen the human story as a drama of the individual soul freely choosing Good or Evil have recognized readily enough that this individual soul may be corrupted by the world. A Christian who prays, "Lead us not into temptation," thereby confesses that what we do may be in part dependent on the circumstances in which we find ourselves. But he does not conclude therefore that the conduct of all men depends on "nothing but" the temptations to which they are exposed.

The social scientist who has observed that gangsters often grow up in the slums and who leaps from that to the conclusion that nothing except the slum environment can have counted in determining the results is making a very large assumption indeed. So far as logical necessity goes he is not compelled to say—as he usually does—that "antisocial behavior" is always the result of individual conditioning. It would be at least as logical to say instead, "Since all men do not always do what my techniques are intended to make them do and the boy who grew up next door to the criminal sometimes turns out to be a reformer instead of a gangster, I therefore assume that certain factors are operative other than those on which my manipulative techniques are based."

When, on the contrary, he explains his failures by saying that they are due simply to a not yet perfected technique or to the presence of conditioning factors somehow overlooked, he may be advancing a tenable hypothesis but he has certainly left the realm of direct evidence for the realm of the hypothetical. He has conclusive evidence to prove only what even the most unqualified believer in free will is ready to grant—namely that men can be influenced. He has not presented evidence to *prove* that all human actions are determined. The possible reasons for believing that some realm of freedom does exist cannot be thus ruled out.

To proceed from the actual evidence accumulated in the laboratory, the sociological clinic and the advertising agency to the inclusive propositions often accepted by "today's thinking," one must accept, not merely the evidence itself, but a whole towering structure of assumptions, inferences, guesses and wild leaps across yawning lacunae.

All the real evidence in favor of mechanistic assumptions is partial. All the arguments against any other assumption are merely negative. They consist in saying only, "I have evidence that the body resembles, in certain respects, a machine; I have evidence also that the mind can, in certain ways and to a certain extent, be conditioned. Therefore I assume that nothing not explicable in mechanist terms exists."

Moreover, even this negative evidence is not so impressive as it is usually assumed to be. Once it has been admitted that human behavior has its mechanical aspects, then it ought to be obvious that these are the aspects which the methods appropriate to the study of a mechanism will most readily reveal. If you study man by the method suited to chemistry, or even if you study him in the light of what you have learned about rats and dogs, it is certainly to be expected that what you discover will be what chemistry and animal behavior have to teach. But it is also not surprising or even significant if by such methods you fail to discover anything else.

When the behavior of lower animals is being investigated, the orthodox biologist constantly warns us that we must be on our guard against "anthropomorphic" interpretations. We are, he says, all too prone to assume that a given action means what it would mean if the animal were human and tend therefore to think of the birds and beasts as much more like human beings than they are. But at least one distinguished student of behavior, Dr. Konrad Lorenz, has called attention to an opposite, equally serious, source of error. And he has named it "mechanomorphism."

When we assume that animals are human we no doubt see human traits which are nonexistent. But when we assume that they are machines we make a mechanistic interpretation which may be equally wide of the mark. It is no easier to read *in* than it is to read *out*. And as really philosophical scientists are coming more and more to realize, the experimenter, the instruments he uses, and the hypotheses which he adopts, are all parts of the experiment and help determine its results. In the broadest possible sense, therefore, the kind of perfect detachment which science once hoped to achieve is impossible.

What many psychologists and social scientists seem to be doing is to denounce as a kind of "anthropomorphism" every attempt to interpret even human behavior on the assumption that men are men; to insist that we should proceed as though they were mere animals at most, even if not mere machines in the end. But how can Anthropos be understood except in anthropomorphic terms? Why should we assume that the mechanomorphic error is not really an error at all?

That nineteenth-century scientist who said that he refused to believe in the soul because "I cannot find it in my test tube" made a singularly foolish remark for the simple reason that a test tube is the last place in which a soul would be likely to be found even if, by chance, it did happen to exist. When the scientist replies to this objection by saying that every science must use the methods at its disposal, and that it cannot be expected to concern itself with anything with which it has no method of dealing, it is a legitimate reply—if no attempt is made to make it go beyond what it actually says. But scientists—who do not always share the infallibility and impartiality attributed to science itself—sometimes do, like the chemist who could not find the soul, go a long way beyond.

As a matter of fact they have developed what may be called a standard technique for going that long way without seeming too obviously to do so. The statement that something "does not exist for the purposes of my science" and the statement "therefore I can never know anything about it" become, no less easily, "what we cannot know anything about does not exist." By that simple process the experimental psychologist can get rid of the whole possibility of a realm of freedom quite as easily as the orthodox Behaviorist got rid of consciousness.

Neither the strength nor the weakness of the modern determinist's position was ever more clearly revealed in a short statement than in a speech by Frazier, the benevolent manipulator of his subjects in Walden Two: "I deny that freedom exists at all. I must deny it—or my program is absurd. You cannot have a science about a subject matter which hops capriciously about. Perhaps we can never *prove* that man isn't free; it's an assumption. But the increasing success of a science of behavior makes it more and more plausible."

Mr. Skinner puts this speech into the mouth of a character and one cannot therefore assume that he takes full responsibility for it. But he must have thought that it at least represented a point of view with which he had a good deal of sympathy and it provides a manageable opportunity to examine the concrete claims and professions of faith which a typical exponent of "today's thinking" will make.

Let us suppose by way of parallel that a theologian should reply, "I affirm that God exists. I must affirm it or my whole program is absurd. You can't have a science of God unless God exists. Perhaps I can never *prove* that He does; it's an assumption. But the long-continued success of religion in dealing with men's souls makes it more and more plausible to say that He does."

Frazier would undoubtedly, and very justifiably, reply that this theologian was simply arguing in a circle. To say that God must exist because I would be talking nonsense if he did not, opens the way to the retort: "That is, my dear sir, precisely what you are doing. By admission you start with an unprovable assumption and you certainly have no right, in the name of either logic or yesterday's thinking, to insist that this assumption is inescapable. By your own admission it is 'plausible' at best and it can be plausible only if (1) you can really show me that you have had 'continuing success' and (2) that the success which you have had is not explicable on the basis of any other assumption."

Yet obviously Frazier's own position is precisely parallel to that of our theologian. Admittedly he is proceeding on an assumption, not on a demonstrated fact, and his argument could be restated something like this: "I desire a Science of Man. Without determinism what I call a science cannot exist. Therefore determinism can be assumed." So far as pure logic goes that is no better than saying, "I desire a philosophical system of ethics; without assuming that man is free there can be no such philosophy of ethics; therefore man is free." But the necessity for a Science of Man in the sense implied by Frazier is no more self-evident than the necessity for a philosophy of ethics and any argument based on the assumption that it is, is again an argument based on *pure* assumption.

Mr. Frazier goes on to add: "I didn't say that behavior is always predictable, any more than weather is always predictable. There are often too many factors to be taken into account. We can't measure them all accurately, and we couldn't perform the mathematical operations needed to make the prediction if we had the measurements." But when he says this he is not only making another assumption—namely, that the unpredictable is nevertheless the determined—but making the very one which physics abandoned when it frankly acknowledged the opposite. The argument "I can't have a Science of Man without believing thus and so" is an argument completely without force unless one takes it for granted both that it is necessary to have such a science and that this science cannot exist if it recognizes something which physicists have been successfully recognizing for more than a generation.

If anything remains of Frazier's argument it is only the pragmatic boast "increasing success." But in what, one may ask, does that success really consist and by what standards is "success" to be judged? For the sake of argument one may grant that the Science of Man has successfully predicted and to some extent determined what the mass audience of the movies and the radio will like. Manufacturers of breakfast foods and lipsticks are enthusiastic about the results achieved. But the successes claimed in, say, education and criminology are not equally obvious. Its methods have been increasingly accepted and used but is it really beyond dispute that the graduate of a high school or a college is better educated than he used to be? On the other hand, it is universally admitted that both juvenile delinquency and adult crime are increasing. Is this in spite of improved scientific methods of combating them? Or is it, as a theologian might argue, *because* of them?

To what indubitable success in dealing with the most intelligent section of the public or with the highest activities of the mind can the Science of Man point? What genius or saint has ever become what he is by being "conditioned" as such? Has any Walden Two, even, been successfully established, and does either the successful conditioning of rats or the successful prediction that more people will listen to a jazz band than to a symphony orchestra give any very convincing proof that it could be?

The very word "success" is highly ambiguous unless somehow one makes it clear whether it is to be taken to mean "achieving limited ends without regard to their value" or "achieving something which we regard as desirable." Frazier uses it in the first sense when he is claiming that certain techniques can be made to work; in the second sense when he implies one of those value judgments which he claims never to make and asks us to surrender ourselves to his techniques because they are "successful" in the sense of promoting the Good Life. Yet the "success" on which his argument finally rests is dubious when dealing with any but the crudest manifestations of human nature; worse than dubious in so far as it implies that the Good Life has been promoted. "Psychology" has taught the merchant that he can charge more for "fat-free milk" than he could if he called it "skimmed," but it has not made it any easier to write a *Hamlet*. Advertising, not culture, is the most characteristic product of the scientific study of the mind on mechanistic principles.

When even a Frazier is compelled to admit that human conduct cannot always be predicted and that the unreality of individual freedom cannot be proved, it is obvious that a readiness to accept a purely mechanistic Science of Man does not rest on any ground more solid than the conviction that its premises are the most probable and the most useful. But if anyone doubts that the validity of such a purely mechanistic Science of Man is still being insisted upon by responsible persons, even outside the social sciences, he may consult a book recently addressed to the uninstructed by Dr. G. Gamow, Professor of Theoretical Physics at George Washington University, entitled *Mr. Tompkins Learns the Facts of Life,* and published by the Cambridge University Press. Defending mechanism, Dr. Gamow writes, "The mechanistic point of view is ... that all phenomena observed in the living organism can be reduced in the end to regular physical laws governing the atoms of which that organism is constructed, and that the difference lies entirely in the relative complexity of living and non-living matter. According to this point of view, basic manifestations of life like *growth, motion, reproduction,* and even *thinking* ... can be accounted for, at least in principle, by the same basic laws of physics which determine ordinary inorganic processes."

While the whole tendency of our generation has been toward a more and more general acceptance of the notion that a mechanism of some sort *must* be the explanation of every social or psychic phenomenon, the tendency has also been to acknowledge at the same time that the supposed mechanism is more complicated and subtle than the first mechanists supposed. Few would now be satisfied to say, as Descartes said in the seventeenth century, that animals "act naturally and by springs like a watch"; or, as the idea was elaborated by Malebranche, that all mere animals "eat without pleasure, they cry without pain, they grow without knowing it; they desire nothing, they fear nothing, they know nothing." Even fewer would accept as adequate the pronouncement of the eighteenth-century psychologist Cabanis that "the brain secretes thought as the liver secretes bile." Yet too many fail to perceive that the overwhelming arguments against any such absurd formulations are not actually removed simply by positing a more and more "subtle" machine whose methods of operation are never clearly explained. As a matter of fact Professor Gamow's position, stripped of its hocus-pocus, is actually almost the same as that of Cabanis.

When, on the other hand, a Skinner brings himself to admit that the science of physics has itself abandoned the theory of absolute determinism, at least so far as the ultimate particles of matter are concerned, he can add only, "This question of microscopic indeterminancy is not awfully relevant here, because if we could do as much with human behavior as the physicist can do with physical nature (in spite of his admission that in the last analysis he isn't quite sure of a number of things), we could make decisions on some very important problems."

So indeed we could. So indeed, alas, we have done. And perhaps the most important of these decisions is the one which Mr. Skinner makes at the same moment that he declares it to be possible—the decision, that is, to regard all social and moral problems as problems of engineering and to treat the possible autonomy of the individual human being in exactly the same way that orthodox physicists treated the unpredictability of the atom—as long as they were able to do so. These physicists disregarded the "freedom of the atom" as a negligible annoyance of no importance so far as the control of the macroscopic aspects of physical nature is concerned; Mr. Skinner suggests that the possible freedom of the individual be disregarded in the same way. In the end, however, the physicist found that he could no longer disregard it, and as everyone now knows, the most concentrated source of power which science has ever released was made accessible, not by the old physics, but by the new, which accepted and studied the very phenomena that the old had dismissed as negligible. Perhaps it may someday turn out that in the microscopic freedom of the individual rather than in the macroscopic predictability and controllability of the mass resides a releasable force as much more powerful than any which the mechanistic psychology can manipulate as the energy within the atom is more powerful than that within the more predictable aggregate called a molecule.

To deny that the hypotheses of either the fictional Frazier or the very real Professor Gamow actually are the most useful for the promotion of a good life or a good society has been the purpose of much that has so far been said in the course of the present discussion. In this section of that discussion it has been suggested also that even the degree of probability claimed for the hypotheses may not be so great as is often assumed. Would any age before our own have been so readily convinced that man is nothing in himself, or would it, above all, have assumed so readily that to doubt his ability to do anything for himself is a useful or helpful doubt?

6

THE STUBBORN FACT
OF CONSCIOUSNESS

In our recent past the two philosophers to achieve in America the greatest prestige among their fellows were William James and Alfred Whitehead. Neither of them accepted simple determinism or simple mechanism. Indeed, none of James's other theoretical positions is better known than his insistence that religious experience is real in some important sense or than his pragmatic "plumping" for the hypothesis of free will which opens the possibility of radical novelty in the universe and rejects the assumption that "with earth's first clay they did the last man knead." James based his belief in free will partly on the contention that the evidence of our consciousness which "feels free" is at least legitimate evidence of ponderable weight, partly on the pragmatic ground that whatever we may say we believe we never find it possible to act on any assumption other than that there are choices open to us.

But whatever the prestige of both James and Whitehead

and whatever the respect with which they were treated, neither really won the day in the popular or the scientific mind. Partly that was because the first seemed too simple, the second too complex. To some, James's purely pragmatic solution of the difficulty seemed a "way out" rather than a genuine solution. To even more, Whitehead's "frames of reference," his attempt to show how even scientific thinking is, after all, only a *way* of thinking, rather than a description of ultimate reality, seemed altogether too difficult to understand. The experimental scientist as well as the layman found it more convenient, if not very consistent, to be pragmatic on some occasions and to talk about "what really is true" on others; to use, as the Frazier of *Walden Two* did, "It works," when he wants to defend the theory that man can be made whatever one wants to make him but to reject the same argument when presented from the other side.

Even the freest intelligences are to some extent influenced by the atmosphere in which they learned to breathe. Most thinking men alive today grew up mentally under the influence of the very discoveries and theories which led ultimately to the impasse many of them have now reached. More often than not, their first awareness that a world of ideas exists, their first realization that they could learn and think and argue for themselves came when they first became aware of what was then called "the scientific world view" as opposed to the perhaps weakly religious and moralistic attitudes which had been unenthusiastically offered them by parents or elementary teachers.

The choice often appeared to them as little more than a choice between what was accepted by those who were mentally active and what was accepted by those who were not. Fact, experiment, and the establishment of laws were all intellectually respectable; nothing else was. Intelligent men who accomplished something occupied themselves with the objective; the realm of the subjective was simply the realm of delusions and dreams. You cannot measure or predict or control it. The idea that it might be autonomous and creative suggests the possibility that the methods which were working everywhere else might not work there. Concern with it was unscientific and therefore unintelligent. Even Freudianism was in the beginning highly suspect because though it spoke reassuringly of the "mechanisms" of neuroses, these mechanisms were not demonstrably correlated with physical peculiarities of the brain. What lesion, it was asked, does an infantile trauma produce?

Inevitably such habits of thought are difficult to break, even when the necessity for breaking them begins to be felt. It is not merely a matter of accepting additional evidence or even additional evidence of a different kind. It seems also to involve acceptance of a logical inconsistency. The brain is part of the body and the body has demonstrably its mechanical aspects. How, if it has, can it possibly have any other? Is it not nonsensical to suppose that it is part (or sometimes) the one thing, part (or at other times) the other?

It would certainly be simpler not to have to face any such paradox but it is better to face even an unresolved paradox than to disregard the evidence which creates it—and *that* is precisely what the thoroughgoing mechanist does. To realize just how strong that disregarded evidence is, all that is really necessary is to break a certain habit of thought, to look for that evidence as persistently as the mechanist has looked for evidence to support his contentions, and to dismiss the mechanist's a priori assumption that only a certain kind of evidence, collected by certain arbitrarily restricted methods, is really valid. There is an Idol of the Laboratory as well as of the Market Place. And we can escape from the errors which it fosters only if we cease to believe that a thing is obviously an illusion unless it can be measured and experimented with by the same methods which have proved useful in dealing with mechanical phenomena.

All we really need to do is to recognize and attend to phenomena of a different sort and among them, especially, the most indubitable of all: namely, to that consciousness and awareness of self which exists vividly and indisputably in each of us, even though attempts to explain or evaluate them baffle the laboratory technician.

It has already been noted in passing that the mechanist who denies the reality of freedom usually finds it convenient to minimize or even deny the reality of mind or, at least, the significance of mental processes. He may do so, as Mr. Skinner, for example, does, only in the relatively simple sense of denying that we have any way of demonstrating that "thought" exists as anything more than the product of what we have been conditioned to do, to like, and to believe. He may also, however, go much further than that and deny that consciousness itself has more than a shadowy existence, which the genuine scientist is justified in dismissing from his consideration. He can propose to study behavior, both animal and human, on the assumption that any attempt to consider its conscious concomitants would be merely confusing. He can then carry his contempt for "the subjective" to the point where he rejects as evidence anything which it alleges and thus insist, not only that without consciousness behavior may be understood, but also that without it this behavior might proceed exactly as it is now seen to do.

The very existence of consciousness seems to irritate him and that irritation is, granted his enterprise, very easy to understand. If anyone not wholly convinced by his demonstrations still suspects that some autonomous power of thought, possibly some power of choosing not completely dependent on conditioning factors, resides anywhere, it would probably reside within the area of consciousness. As long as that area has not been conclusively demonstrated to be some sort of illusion, even the ultramechanist unwillingly suspects that his demonstration is not so complete as he would like to be. So long as the human machine even thinks that it is thinking, so long as it is capable of even the delusion of free will, it is capable of something of which no mechanism is demonstrably capable. The first and most obvious reason that most people have thought that they were to some extent free is simply that they seemed in their consciousness to be so.

That debate which was staged during the second half of the nineteenth century between the mechanists and the humanists, between the determinists and the believers in some minimal freedom for the human being, was lost and won because of the egregious tactical error which the humanists made when they permitted the issue to depend on the existence of the "soul," instead, as it might well have been made to depend, on the existence of consciousness. The tactical error was fatal not merely or even chiefly because the concept of the "soul" was so closely identified with theological dogma and associated with mythologies which science really could expose as such. More important is the fact that whereas the soul is difficult to define, much less to demonstrate, "consciousness" is self-evident and yet as difficult to reconcile with complete mechanism as the soul itself.

Tactically, the error thus consisted in resting the case on the maximum rather than the minimum requirements of the debate. It permitted the chemist to say, "I cannot find the soul in my test tube," without exposing clearly the fallacy of his argument. If he had been compelled to say instead, "I cannot find consciousness in my test tube," the reply would be simple: "I don't care whether you can find it there or not. I can find it in my head. Chemistry,

by failing to find it, demonstrates nothing except the limitations of its methods. I am conscious, and until you show
me a machine which is also conscious I shall continue to
believe that the difference between me and a mechanism
is probably very significant; even perhaps that what I find
in that consciousness is better evidence concerning things
to which consciousness is relevant than the things which
you find in a test tube." The subjective may be suspect,
but it furnishes at least the only possible entry into a realm
which may exist only in the mind but which certainly
does exist there.

No other power, quality, or attribute—not even free will
or the ability to recognize that one thing is more valuable
or "better" than another—seems less probable in connection with the animal body (which certainly is partly mechanical) or with a brain which is certainly part of the
body. No paradox involving a machine which reasons,
makes choices, and acts autonomously; a machine which
can on occasion be a cause not merely a result; which can
create as well as be influenced or obey laws—is more difficult to resolve than the paradox of a machine which is
conscious. Yet the body machine (if you insist on calling
it that) indubitably is conscious and by so being it effectively disposes of any merely a priori reasons for refusing
to believe that it might also be capable of exhibiting phenomena no more difficult to understand in terms of physics, chemistry, or even logic, than is simple consciousness
itself.

No wonder that mechanists avert their attention from

it. No wonder that they begin by preferring to disregard its existence when they undertake to study behavior in mechanistic terms or that they end by calling it insulting names like "epiphenomenon" and come as close to denying its existence as their own awareness that they are conscious will permit them to come. Yet actually, of course, consciousness is the *only* thing of which we have direct evidence, and to say "I *think* therefore I am" is a statement which rests more firmly on direct evidence than the behaviorists' formula "I *act* therefore I am." After all, it is only because man is conscious that he can know or think he knows that he acts. What he minimizes really comes first and on it everything else rests. What the mechanist disparagingly calls "the subjective" is not that of which we are least, but rather that of which we are *most* certain.

As C. G. Jung once asked, "How on earth do people know that the only reality is the physical atom, when this cannot be proved to exist at all except by means of the psyche? If there is anything which can be described as primary, it must be the psyche, certainly not in any circumstances the atom, which, like everything else in our experience, is only directly given as a model or picture." How, one may add, can the consciousness be dismissed as an epiphenomenon when only by virtue of this epiphenomenon could it be perceived to be an epiphenomenon— or anything else.

Once what cannot be effectively denied is effectually admitted, a whole universe which exists in consciousness, even if it exists nowhere else, demands recognition. At a minimum, this new universe includes the whole realm of sensation, which must be admitted to be in some sense real by anyone who has ever pricked his finger or had the toothache, but which is as impossible as the soul itself to "find in a test tube." Even the most elementary textbooks of physics are careful to point out that neither sound nor color can be said to exist "objectively"; that what physics recognizes as waves in the air and used to call waves in the ether until it stopped believing that ether exists, cannot in any way be equated with what we know directly as sound or light.

Undoubtedly there are good reasons for distinguishing the "objective" from the "subjective" phenomena when our purpose is to study the first. But there is no justification whatsoever for calling only the one real. That realm of reality which consists of undulating air, and that realm which consists not merely of sound but also of music and all that music implies, may seem discontinuous with each other or at least continuous in some way which our minds have never been able to understand. But if the reality of the one or the other is to be denied, then it ought to be admitted that it can be only the inferred realm of air waves, not the self-evident realm of sensations, which is dubious.

Once the reality of the realm of sensation has been admitted, it is difficult not to admit a great deal more. The realm of the consciousness is not composed exclusively of sensations. In it there somehow exist also the emotions which even sound or color can provoke when they are arranged in certain ways by composers or painters. So too do Pride and Guilt and Shame. So too do Logic and Discourse—even of the sort used to demonstrate that they can have no significance. And if such improbable things are indubitably found in that realm, then it would perhaps be there—if anywhere—that the autonomy of the human being who is conscious might also be found. At least not finding them anywhere else is not conclusive proof that they do not exist, and if the refusal to look for them there means anything, it means only that the seekers are determined in advance not to expose themselves to the risk of being finders also.

The problem of the apparent discontinuity between the two realms still remains. How a material body can be aware of sensations is perhaps the thorniest of all metaphysical problems. It is as hard to imagine how we get from one realm to the other, what is the connection between the world of things and the world of sensations— let alone between the world of things and that of thoughts and emotions—as it is to imagine how one might manage to enter the mathematician's world of the fourth dimension. But there is a vast difference also. Actually we can't, or at least have never been able to, get into the fourth dimension. But we undoubtedly do have a large part of our being in the realm of the consciousness. The physical body does think and feel. Much as the physical scientist may hate to admit what he cannot account for, this fact he can hardly deny. The seemingly impossible is the most indisputably true.

From the dilemma posed by the phenomenon, "a conscious machine," there is only one possible escape and that is through a realization that such categories as "material—immaterial" or "mechanical—not mechanical" are not as inevitable or as mutually exclusive as we think; that the "either or" assumption can involve a fallacy analogous with that of the "nothing but." A machine which is conscious simply cannot be placed in the category "machine," as that category was established by common sense, originally for its own use and convenience. To call a machine which thinks a "machine" nevertheless, is to extend the term to a degree which makes it actually meaningless, and when you say "everything is mechanical" you are not really saying anything since you cannot establish a class if no other class exists. No "either or" is valid unless the reference is to mutually exclusive categories, and the existence of consciousness in a machine is sufficient proof that in this case "mechanical" and "not mechanical" are not such categories. Above all, you have no right to say "consciousness and thought obey mechanical laws" when it is obvious that you no longer know what "mechanical" means.

Once common sense has accepted a pair of categories, it has great difficulty in realizing that they may have no absolute validity and that the time may come when they have to be abandoned. Yet the history of common-sense practices, as well as the history of science itself, is full of instances where this is exactly what happened.

Consider for instance the striking and spectacular example which happens to involve very recent discoveries and concerns a pair of categories which seem obviously fundamental, namely the matter-energy dichotomy. To have said to any nineteenth-century scientist that a thing was not necessarily either matter or energy but that it might be now one and now the other would have seemed the merest nonsense. Common sense saw the distinction as primary and self-evident; scientific experiments confirmed it and scientific laws were based on it. Yet the concept of matter-energy is now universally accepted as a concept superseding the former one. Matter which may turn itself into energy is not "material" in any older meaning of the word. Similarly a machine which can be aware of itself is no longer "mechanical" in any meaningful sense of the word.

Even closer—indeed so intimately related that in the end it comes down to the same thing—is the parallel with the problem which has faced the biologist ever since he began to be aware that the theory of evolution evoked paradoxes almost at the very moment when it seemed to be explaining away the last possible objections to an inclusive and exclusive interpretation of the universe in mechanistic terms. As everyone knows, Darwin's great contributions to a theory which had been repeatedly if tentatively advanced during the whole century preceding him were two: he collected a vast number of specific facts which indicated that evolution actually had taken place and—what is much more important—he suggested "natural selection" as a *mechanism* by means of which evolutionary changes might be produced.

The noun deserves to be italicized because the concept of "natural selection" does not require the intervention of any will, intention, purpose, intelligence, or consciousness —whether they be human, natural or divine. It is genuinely mechanistic and deterministic because it suggests that things must be exactly what they are, that they could not possibly be otherwise. If most of the rationalists before Darwin's time who rejected religious tradition nevertheless called themselves deists rather than either atheists or even agnostics, that was largely because they did not see how the universe, particularly the universe of living creatures, could have simply happened. Evidences of design were too obvious and Lucretius' blind chance did not seem to account for them because chance could never lead to direct growth and seemingly purposeful change. Theology's last resort, the "proof of the existence of God" which survived both belief in revelation and trust in the infallibility of metaphysics, was the one summed up in the sentence, "The existence of a watch presupposes the existence of a watchmaker"; and it carried the day. But Darwin seemed to have swept it away at last. Natural selection, while remaining a purely mechanical process, could nevertheless imitate intention as Lucretius' pure chance could not. It seemed to explain how, given sufficient time, the watch could make itself.

For a time and not unpardonably many believed that the last mystery had been explained; that our world had become a completely daylight world fully comprehensible in common-sense terms and that the whole history of life, almost the whole history of the universe itself, could now be written with assurance. Taken up by minds more aggressive, more impetuous, and perhaps more arrogant than Darwin's, his theory became, in the hands of Huxley, Ernst Haeckel and the latter's even less cautious disciples, the basis of even more sweeping deductions. The grand scheme of nature was said to be one which we must accept without attempting to intervene. Translate "with earth's first clay—" into something like "the first amoeba inevitably leads, through a series of unbreakable necessities, to both Shakespeare and Darwin," and they believed it to be true.

Today, on the other hand, by no means all biologists are anything like so certain that they know all the significant facts, much less the remoter ethical conclusions to be drawn from them. That is partly because the logic behind the supposed certitudes has been more carefully examined and partly because the number of known facts has been enormously increased. With the passage of time the theory of evolution has been, in so far as it is merely a description of something which happened, far more conclusively established than it was in Darwin's time. But the mechanism, if mechanism is an adequate word, has come to seem far more complex than it was originally supposed and the remote philosophical and ethical deductions far less clear than they seemed. Moreover, this increased assurance that evolution has taken place, coupled with a decreased assurance that we understand fully either "how" or "why," has developed principally within biology itself, and is in no way dependent on such primarily metaphysical objections as those popularized by Bergson and enthusiastically championed by Bernard Shaw.

Almost the whole science of genetics, almost everything which is known about "the mechanism of heredity," is post-Darwinian. When it had been definitely demonstrated, as most biologists outside the Iron Curtain countries agree that it has been, that acquired characteristics cannot be inherited, the process of natural selection is deprived of its most easily understandable supply of variations from which natural process may choose, and it is now believed to have to rely on spontaneous novelties called "mutations." Thus even though all this may also be reduced to the status of a mechanism, it is at least a much more complicated mechanism than the one originally assumed, and it again seems to make everything depend on chance, though chance is never a wholly comfortable concept for those who want to keep the machine thoroughly mechanical. Under what appears to be "chance" may just possibly lurk all sorts of things neither accounted for nor understood.

Because the biologists, like the physicists, are often less naïve than the psychologists and the sociologists, they have raised fundamental questions and realized their implications. In one way or another, this has often led them to admit the possibility that the intervention of mind—which may have made its first appearance in the universe during the course of terrestrial evolution—introduces a new factor capable of originating changes of its own. The most positive and downright formulation of this concept is that which took the name of "emergent evolution," and the most immediate and practical conclusion drawn from it was that since conscious purpose has now emerged man is now, and to a considerable extent, at least able to direct evolution and to become what he wants to be rather than necessarily what "natural selection," indifferent to his conscious wishes, would inevitably make him. For the inscrutable and probably random purposeless "purpose" of nature can now be substituted the conscious purpose of mankind, which has set its own standards of value and can act in accordance with them whether they are or are not recognized by anything outside man himself.

Like most pat phrases, "emergent evolution," has its dangers. Like "the survival of the fittest," it may be invoked as a sort of magic formula and used, not as an aid in the examination of a knotty question, but in order to dismiss it. For that reason many biologists hesitate to use the phrase even though they may cautiously recognize the reality behind the phenomena which it almost too conveniently sums up. Their very caution nevertheless gives greater weight to their admission that certain phenomena do elude simple mechanistic explanations and one may find such phenomena very succinctly described in the recent writings of, for example, Julian Huxley—a distinguished biologist in his own right as well as a scholar continuously abreast of the work of others.

To begin with, Huxley recognizes that, however inconvenient the reality of consciousness and the other manifestations of mind may be to anyone who wishes to give a simple account of the way things work; however much less complicated the history of life would be without them; however difficult it may be to grasp the relationship between them and the chemical-physical processes—the fact remains that they do exist. As he puts it in his very recent *Evolution in Action*:

The impulses which travel up to the brain along the nerves are of an electrical nature and differ only in their time relations, such as their frequency, and in their intensity. But in the brain, these purely quantitative differences in electrical pattern are translated into wholly different qualities of sensation. The miracle of mind is that it can transmute quantity into quality. This property of mind is something given: it just is so. It cannot be explained: it can only be accepted.

The evolutionary biologist, functioning as such, can do no more than trace the development in time of the mechanism of the brain and of its connection with the elusive mental phenomena that occur. But even as biologist he cannot deny either that they do occur or that they are not completely understandable in terms of the biological developments which undoubtedly do keep step, as it were, with

131

them. "Mental activity is intensified and mental organization improved during evolution."

Moreover, the whole significance of Huxley's position will be missed if it is not clearly perceived that it is scarcely less different from that of the mechanist than it is from either the theories of the "vitalists" or the simplest theological doctrine of the "soul." The "Life" of the vitalist and "the spirit" of the theologian are separate, discontinuous entities temporarily inhabiting a machine. To the mere mechanist, on the other hand, what are commonly called "mind" and "psyche" are "nothing but" the machine itself. But to Huxley and to many—perhaps to most present-day biologists—the relationship is far more intimate than religion or vitalism commonly assumes, even though this relationship is by no means describable in terms of a "nothing but." To understand it requires something like that breaking down of categories with which we were a few moments ago concerned. Some realization is required of the fact that "the material" and "the mechanical" include potentialities which render meaningless the ordinary understanding of what the categories "material" and "mechanical" imply.

On the one hand Huxley writes, "Mind is not an entity in its own right, and our minds are not little separate creatures inhabiting our skulls. . . . Mental activity, as the past hundred years of research have clearly shown, is tied in with cerebral activity." On the other hand: "Mind is not a pale epiphenomenon, not a mere 'ghost in the machine,' to use Professor Ryle's phrase, but an *operative* part of life's mechanism. . . . For a biologist, much the easiest way is to think of mind and matter as two aspects of a single, underlying reality—shall we call it world substance, the stuff out of which the world is made. At any rate, this fits more of the facts and leads to fewer contradictions than any other view. In this view, mental activities are among the inevitable properties of world substance when this is organized in the form of the particular kind of biological machinery we find in a brain."

Moreover—but as mechanistically inclined evolutionists are strangely unable to see—the theory that consciousness is a shadowy epiphenomenon and not, to use Huxley's word, "operative" at all, is actually inconsistent with the theory of natural selection itself. For if natural selection does not maintain or further develop characteristics which have no survival value, then why should it have gone on developing higher and higher degrees of consciousness? Why, above all, should it have produced and then infinitely elaborated the most elusive aspects of consciousness, such as those which involve a conviction of autonomy and the making of value judgments which do not seem to be those of "nature"? Why and by what process could natural selection foster the unreal and the useless?

Because he raises some such questions as these, Huxley is led to conclude:

"For the modern biologist, the dialectical materialism that provides the philosophical basis for Marxist communism is an erroneous survival from days before the principles of evolution were properly understood. . . . We shall get nowhere without intensive study of physiology and material structure and observable behavior; but unless we combine this with introspection, interpretation, and deduction from subjective experience, we shall not get very far, as the fate of the Behaviorist movement shows. . . ."

Perhaps it would be something more than an exercise in verbalism to say that in the course of evolution the epiphenomenon consciousness—if it was once only that—"emerged" as a phenomenon in its own right.

From the positions taken by the early mechanistic evolutionists to such statements as Huxley finds it necessary to make is a long way. Biology has, he says, "until quite recently," tended to minimize the difference between the animal and the human being. "This is partly because we have often been guilty of the fallacy of mistaking origins for explanations. If sexual impulse is at the base of love, then love is to be regarded as nothing but sex; if it can be shown that man originated from an animal, then in all essentials he is nothing but an animal. . . . We have tended to misunderstand the nature of the difference between ourselves and animals. We have a way of thinking that if there is a continuity in time there must be a continuity in quality." Mind has, he believes, now been projected "into the business of evolution." Though perhaps the powers of mind could not help coming into existence they also cannot help "becoming operative factors for further change. Thus, once life had become organized in human form it was impelled forward, not merely by the blind forces of natural selection but by mental and spiritual forces as well."

One part of this is, of course, not only accepted but emphasized by such a mechanist as the fictional Frazier. He proposes to become, in one sense, an operational factor in evolution by "conditioning" his victims in accordance with what have become for him "self-evident" ideals. On the other hand he refuses to acknowledge the qualitative novelty which consciousness introduces and which, once it is introduced, suggests the possibility of some sort of autonomy for him as well as for those whom he wishes to manipulate mechanistically. He rejects the whole concept of radical novelty in the universe. Even consciousness must be explained away. For him life is "nothing but" chemistry; the brain "nothing but" a machine by which reflex actions can be "learned" only in the sense that electronic calculating machines can "learn" what their manipulators want them to. Presumably chemistry is older than life; presumably reflex action is an older characteristic of living things than the power of conscious thought. Therefore he assumes it to be probable that nothing but chemistry and reflex action can possibly exist.

Actually, it is not really so much because the mechanical aspects of the human being are older—after all man has been familiar with his consciousness and with his ability to make decisions longer than he has been familiar with almost anything else—as it is because they are *simpler,* that we find them both easier to believe in and easier to use for limited experimental purposes than any of the qualitatively different phenomena. If only, the Fraziers say, we refuse to take into consideration consciousness and all that goes with it, we can confidently plan our Walden Two and we can also feel confident that we understand the universe fully, completely, and without very much mental effort.

Grant him his "if" and there is much to be said for his attitude. Within the field to which the mechanist voluntarily but stubbornly restricts himself there is, for obvious reasons, nothing which simple mechanistic concepts cannot account for. The categories which long familiarity have made to seem inevitable from any common-sense viewpoint are adequate. We do not have to trouble ourselves about the mechanism which exhibits capacities not mechanical; we do not have to come close to the borders of the conceivable by attempting to understand how what is not mechanical can be related to what is. Above all, we do not have to admit that there are paradoxes which we cannot clearly resolve; that certain things appear to be compatible though we do not quite see how they can be. We are not compelled to say of anything, as Huxley says of the mind's power to translate quantitative differences in electrical impulses into qualitatively different kinds of sensation, "This property of mind is something given: it just is so."

The refusal to accept too readily something which seems inconsistent with our previous experiences, to resist the impulse to say too often or too promptly, "We bow the head and do not understand," is laudable enough. Of course it is true that, in one sense, nothing is ever understandable. The existence of matter is as much a mystery as the existence of mind, and of the atom, no less than of consciousness, we may have ultimately to say only that it is "something given." But what rational "explanation" really means is the attempt to reduce the number of things which "just are so" by relating them one to another and attempting to see how one implies the other. That is what the rationalists were doing when they tried to describe the phenomena associated with mind in terms of those properties of matter which they had already accepted as among the things which "just are." They did not want to have to say of anything else, "Here is something not implied by what we have already accepted but which is also 'just so.'" But what the situation now has come down to seems to be simply this: Either we must acknowledge the existence of the category which includes all the mental phenomena somehow associated with the physical and the chemical in a way which is by no means clear; or we must, like the mechanists, simply say that these phenomena do not really exist because everything which cannot be demonstrated to be the direct result of physical and chemical process must be mere "ghosts in the machine" or mere "epiphenomena."

Against this last alternative it can be said that it requires a lot of resolute blindness to dismiss "mind" as a shadow, and a lot of faith in very fragmentary demonstrations, to

E*   137 explain human experience as well as human conduct without any recognition of consciousness and what consciousness seems to imply. Against the acceptance of the new category which includes machines that have ceased to be mechanical as well as such realities as consciousness and autonomy, it can be said only that it implies an admission that what we cannot understand clearly is nevertheless true; that living creatures, especially the living human being, present paradoxes we do not know how to resolve.

It would, of course, be a pity if we escaped from the practical consequences of materialist determinism and the absurdities which it involves only to relapse into solipsism or into what must have been the seemingly hapless situation of primitive man when he felt that almost everything was a separate mystery and that therefore almost anything might be true. But it is now really unnecessary to choose between saying, "We can understand nothing," and "Whatever I cannot understand must be untrue." There is a middle position which consists in saying that the human mind has established a genuine contact with reality but that there is not yet—possibly never will be—a perfect correspondence between the categories of our understanding, between the concepts which we use in thinking and the universe itself.

This, as we shall presently see, is actually the position which many scientists, especially physicists, are tending increasingly to take. Moreover, the refusal of mechanists to entertain it involves an odd inconsistency very much like others already pointed out. We might have supposed that those who deny autonomous power to the mind, who insist that it is "nothing but" the product of the conditioning influences which have been brought to bear upon it, would be the first to admit that the mind is not omnicompetent. Yet those who do insist that the mind is capable of no more than organizing behavior responses are the very ones who say, "What is not completely understandable and does not seem perfectly consistent to this very limited mind cannot possibly be real or true."

Of the "middle ground" and what practical as well as theoretical advantages there are in taking our position on it, more will presently be said. First, however, it might be well to look briefly at two exhibits of which mechanistic determinists have made much. One is an instrument of analysis; the other is a gadget. They are, respectively, statistical predictability and the electronic pseudo-brain.

7

HOW PROBABLE IS PROBABILITY?

Some years ago an ingenious journalist filled his column with speculation about the people who would jump from the Brooklyn Bridge during the twelve months to come. At the moment probably none of them knew that he was going to do anything of the kind. Probably at the moment each would have been appalled by the fate in store for him. But somebody would be compelled to jump because statistics prove that somebody always does.

When the time came each would suppose that he had his private reasons. But the real reason would be that the Law must be obeyed. The question is merely: Who will be picked out by the God of Mathematics to demonstrate His infallibility? Will it be, perhaps, you or I? In any event it will be some of us, and the number will be not much larger or much smaller than usual. Figures don't lie and some will have to be sacrificed to prove that they do not.

Presumably most of the journalist's readers saw the joke and smiled, but it is less likely that very many realized just why the jest was so good. He was pointing his finger at a paradox which has come, in our day, to have enormous practical importance and philosophical significance. This is the Age of Statistics as well as the Age of Anxiety, and statistics furnish a set of tools without the use of which the theory that men are predictable and controllable machines would be very difficult to maintain. No mechanist claims that he can either foresee or determine what an individual man will do. At most he asserts that he can determine and foresee in terms of an average.

But how and to what extent are we bound by such averages? If, for instance, a new bridge is built and more people jump, does that mean that you or I are somehow compelled to do our part toward keeping up the new average? Whether or not God's foreknowledge is incompatible with free will is a very old problem. The statistician has invented a new kind of foreknowledge. He is, indeed, a new kind of god. Does that raise a new problem? Or does it settle the old one once and for all?

The very idea of compiling statistics and the very notion that they may mean something are relatively new though both may now seem to us to be inevitable. One Sir William Petty who published in 1691 a book with the engaging title *Political Arithmetic* is said to have been the first Englishman to see the possibilities of the statistical method as applied to the investigation of social phenomena. He compared, for instance, the average mortality rate for patients admitted to hospitals in London and in Paris, and it seems to have occurred to no one before him that this might throw some light on the question which was the better managed. A good many people, including Samuel Pepys, sensed the originality of his investigations but few can have guessed that we should come in time to live by averages more truly than we can be said to live by anything else.

In Sir William's time men were already in hot pursuit of the "laws" of nature. The assumption that her phenomena were dependably regular and could be described in mathematical formulae had already taken possession of the mind. Newton was in mid-career. But it was the precise, the dependable, the inevitable which engaged the attention. It was with what *always* happens that science, or the New Learning, seemed destined to concern itself, and it was the idea of the certain, not of the probable, that excited the mind.

Mathematically that meant the concept of "function." A equals B, or twice B, or B squared, or perhaps, even, the instantaneous rate of variation of B with respect to C. But whatever A is equal to it is always and precisely equal. One value is tied to the other directly and unchangeably and the description of this relationship constitutes a "law of nature." The idea of a "law" which is only sometimes true, of a relationship which exists and yet cannot be formulated in such a way as to make prediction more than a probability is something quite different. It is less easy to understand metaphysically or to apply for practical purposes. Even the most eminent mathematicians are not in agreement.

As a matter of fact—and this is the point which really concerns us—in every case where a "law" can be stated only in terms of statistical averages two possible interpretations present themselves. One is that the uncertainty involved is simply the result of partial ignorance. Perhaps the data on which we base our prediction is inaccurate or perhaps we are considering only some of the factors which determine the result. Naturally, therefore, we are sometimes wrong, either because the inaccuracy is gross or because the factor we are not taking into account is, in this instance, of paramount importance.

A plant, let us say, usually blooms after the sun has shone on it for a certain number of hours. This year it doesn't. But that is because there has been a very abnormal lack of rainfall, and we were wrong in our prediction simply because we were basing it on the single factor which is usually decisive. But we may, nevertheless, be right in our assumption that definite factors produce definite results. On this interpretation a statistical law is simply one which has not been fully formulated or applied.

This is, of course, the interpretation usually given and the one which the present set of our minds predisposes us to accept. It is what the Frazier of Walden Two had in mind when he protested: "I didn't say that behavior is always predictable, any more than the weather is always predictable. There are often too many factors to be taken into account. We cannot measure them all accurately, and we couldn't perform the mathematical operations needed to make the prediction if we had the measurements." Frazier was, in other words, sure that everything is determined, even though he does not even hope that everything will someday be predictable. Thus, though he admits a limit to the knowable, he will not consider even the possibility that anything may be indeterminate.

If you ask him how he can be sure that what is admittedly forever unpredictable is nevertheless ineluctably determined, he will answer only that it would be very inconvenient to assume anything else. He is committed, as all physical scientists once were, to belief in the fixed order of nature. That means that even the word "chance" is useful only as a way of referring to what happens within an area where the determining factors are unknown to us and that the concept of "freedom" is logically absurd. You cannot, as he protested, have a science if things "hop about," and he has resolved to have a science. The "proof" that this is a universe which never violates a "natural law" is simply that you have assumed that it is.

There is, nevertheless, another possible meaning for some part of the margin of error in statistical predictions. It is less easy to grasp, almost impossible to formulate. But in the physical sciences it is today almost universally accepted and it frankly assumes that an element of uncertainty is not necessarily the result of imperfect knowledge or of imperfect method but may be the consequence of the primary fact that the *unpredictable* and the *indeterminate* are part of ultimate reality.

Now one might have expected that the observers of human behavior would have been the first to suggest this seemingly desperate conclusion. If they reject it, they are compelled to disregard the whole difficulty of reconciling human experience with the supposed laws of behavior. Yet it was the physicist, who faced no such difficulty, who first came to see that statistics do not really mean what they were taken to mean. It was the physicist who first realized what the sociologist frequently denies, namely that statistical results are *merely* statistical, and that no fully determining laws are operating.

This conclusion was not easily arrived at because the long habit of the scientific age—perhaps even something in the structure of the human mind—makes it very difficult not to think exclusively in terms of efficient causes and their necessary effects. The concept of the ultimately random, much more the concept of "freedom" or of a causeless cause, is very difficult to grasp. Until quite recently, therefore, the physical sciences saw no reason to struggle with the problem of the random which was assumed to be only the result of causes too complex to be analyzed. But they have come at last to admit that this interpretation does not always fit the facts.

Unexpected and disconcerting as this admission seems to be there had long existed a background of metaphysical skepticism which might have prepared the scientific mind for it if the scientific mind had not previously decided to pay no attention to metaphysics. As a matter of fact the fundamental assumption concerning the universal reign of cause and effect had hardly become the accepted basis of popular as well as scientific thought when the background of skepticism—long kept in the background—began to form. Hume questioned whether the nexus between so-called cause and so-called effect could ever be shown actually to exist; whether we ever really knew more than that one thing had followed another in time; and whether, therefore, the whole concept of cause might not be simply an attempt on the part of the human mind to read into the external world what was actually no more than the mind's way of thinking.

Before the end of the nineteenth century Karl Pearson attempted, even in a popular book, to introduce the layman to the notion that the "physical laws" to which everything was supposed to be reducible are actually only a fiction. What is called Science is, he said, merely another name for History. It is merely an account of what has happened, accompanied by the hope that it may be expected to happen again or, as he might have put it but did not, that the so-called demonstrations of science are actually only analogous to "the lessons of history." They are, in other words, the best thing we have to go on in forming expectations but they are by no means certainties. And it is significant that Pearson should have been a mathematician especially concerned with statistical probabilities and that he should have devised the still fundamental formula for determining the "coefficient of correlation" by which we attempt to measure the degree of dependence exhibited by a phenomenon which is somehow related to, but not completely determined by, another.

Until the "New Physics" was launched—perhaps with Clerk-Maxwell and his individual molecules, not all of which obey the "law" supposed to govern their motions—Hume's skepticism and even Pearson's irritating unorthodoxy could be dismissed as mere perverse metaphysical ingenuities which the realistic need not take seriously. But when, as has now been proved the case, the assumption that if you have the complete data you can be sure what is going to happen breaks down even in the laboratory; when even an individual atom becomes as unpredictable as the individual man who may or may not jump off the Brooklyn Bridge—then even practical men have to reconsider their premises.

The physicist, no less than Frazier, finds it very disconcerting to discover that the particles with which he has to deal "hop about." In fact the Quantum Theory is a theory dealing with this hopping about. But unlike Frazier he does not react by stubbornly asserting that, at least for practical purposes, it may be assumed that they don't. Reluctantly perhaps, but step by step nevertheless, the concept of strict determinism is abandoned by the physicists. Most of them now admit that when we can predict only average, not individual, behavior, that is, sometimes at least, because of the factors introduced by either free or random elements, not simply because our data or our formulae are incomplete.

From this it is only a step to the denouement of the whole comic drama of determinism, to that final reversal of fortune which takes place when the whole situation is seen to have been previously misconceived. *All* laws, say some physicists, are merely statistical laws, merely expression of a probability based on averages. *Nothing* can be predicted except in the same sense and subject to the same limitations as the number of suicides can be. Therefore the fact that some behavior—that of human beings for example—can be studied only statistically does not mean merely that the methods are, or must remain, imperfect. It means that nothing can be studied in any other way and that it is in the case of what was supposed to be completely predictable that we have been misled by ignorance and the incompleteness of our data. When we do know enough, as we have recently come to know enough about the atom, we perceive that what was taken to be a dependable law has become merely a matter of statistical probability.

Instead of hoping that many subjects now susceptible to no more than this sort of statistical study will in time have their unbreakable laws reduced to definite formulation we may have to admit instead that no subject ever has been so reduced. The ultimate fact about the universe is not that everything in it obeys a law but that the random, or at least the unpredictable, is always present and effective. Newton's assumption that every particle of matter in the universe behaves thus or so is certainly wrong, and we should at least remember that no prediction frankly based on the kind of statistical "laws" which govern the behavior of groups of separately observable individuals is ever dependably accurate. There is always an irreducible margin of error. And that is true whether one is dealing with potential suicides or merely with the toss of a coin.

Mathematicians have long struggled with the mathematical meaning of "probability" without fully illuminating it in connection with even so simple a subject as this last. So baffling is it to mere common sense that the average man, matching for drinks at a bar, still usually acts as though he believed that another "heads" is less probable if the last three tosses have turned out thus, and he continues to act on that "hunch" even though he knows that neither theory nor experiment confirm his instinct.

The more times the coin is tossed the more "probable" it is that the number of heads and tails will be nearly equal. It is because of an easy extension of this "law" that most of even honest roulette wheels pay the operator off in the course of time—though the fact remains that the man who broke the bank is not a mere legend. In a popular article Waldemar Kaempffert cites the case when, in 1931, a ball at Monte Carlo fell into a black pocket twenty-six times in succession despite the fact that the mathematical chances against this are said to be 67 million to 1. Nobody can say that any finite number of tossed coins will infallibly produce an equal number of heads and tails. Nobody can say that 67 million spins of the roulette wheel certainly will produce a run of twenty-six blacks.

With desperate ingenuity the mathematicians take another step. They calculate what they call "the mean variation," or what we might prefer to describe as the "probability of probability." They calculate, for instance, what is likely to be the average deviation from a perfectly equal distribution of heads and tails if you make a hundred throws, a thousand, or ten thousand. But the mean deviation is itself only the *mean*. It is not always the same for a given number of tosses. The element of unpredictability is still there and one might, no doubt, go on to calculate, not merely the probability of probability, but the probability that in any given case the "mean variation" will be exactly realized, or what, in other words, is the probability of the probability of probability.

But the random can never be entirely disposed of. And if the statistician argues that nothing can be called random if it can be shown to obey a law we may reply that nothing can be called a law which does not always work. Heads might sometimes fall a hundred times in succession and the statistician can only tell you how many million tossings you must be prepared to make in order to reach the "probability" that one of them would give you an unbroken succession of heads. Even he will not assure you that that many—or twice that many—would *guarantee* such a series.

The social scientist grows arrogant because of the success of his statistical predictions in dealing with something far more complicated than either the toss of a coin or the behavior of a gaseous molecule. He ought to be, but usually is not, far more aware than the physicist of the whole dubious nature of even physical "laws." What he is trying to do is to watch the behavior of human beings as the physicist watches that of atoms and molecules. He tries, or thinks he tries, to detach himself as far as possible; to treat what he knows about himself as though it were as irrelevant as self-knowledge used to be assumed to be for the natural scientist; and he tries to put himself at a sufficient distance so that nothing but the movements of the aggregate can be seen. But he ought not hope to prove what many physicists now admit is not only unprovable but false.

In order to understand what this means, let us imagine an intruder from Mars totally ignorant of earthly human nature and suspended above our earth at just the point which will enable him to perceive mass movements. It is a sweltering day in August and his attention is attracted to the area of metropolitan New York. From the center of the city long lines are streaming out toward the sea and converging at various points on what we call the shore of Long Island. The Martian observer is a competent one. He has witnessed this phenomenon on various other occasions and has carefully noted the circumstances which surround it. By now he is ready to announce a law: Whenever the temperature rises above a certain point the stream begins to flow and the higher the temperature, the heavier the stream. He has not yet plotted the curve which will give an approximate formula to express the relation between temperature and magnitude of movement. It obviously will not be a straight line because the temperature effect increases as it rises toward a certain point and then declines again. But that can wait. It is obvious now that, almost as surely as an apple falls, thousands of people go to Coney Island when it gets hot.

His law is dependable enough to be relied on for practical purposes by all who are responsible for any kind of vehicular traffic. Meanwhile, however, you and I may stay at home. However inexorable the general law is presumed to be, it is by no means certain that any given individual will obey it. You and I decide, or seem to ourselves to decide, whether or not we will do our part in making the law hold.

Everyone, even among those most bedazzled by statistics, is ready enough to admit this. But what, inquire the statisticians, can this possibly mean except that we who stay at home have our actions determined by factors not operative upon others. Yet if this is true, then why does the proportion of people acted upon by special factors remain so nearly constant? Is no individual really bound to the law or is each of us bound to it, though only to the extent that we must not and cannot exercise our freedom often enough to upset the average?

If this last states the real fact then we are faced with something less clearly defined and more difficult to understand than either the concept of determinism or the concept of freedom. And this is, as a matter of fact, precisely what we *are* faced with both in physics and sociology. Karl

Pearson, among others, has faced it squarely, and what his position seems to come down to is simply this: an individual is free, but the group of which he is a part is not. Any given man's destiny is to some extent in his own hands; but the destiny of mankind is predetermined. You or I may really refuse to go to Coney Island; but a great many people certainly will go.

If this really is true, it means for the individual at least something. It means that so far as his personal conduct and his personal life are concerned he may really and effectively behave as though he were endowed with free will; that in fact, as an individual, he is. It relieves him of the kind of despair which settles on many men when they accept what they have been increasingly taught, namely that they are simply the product of their time and their circumstances. It means, even, that a Thoreau was not simply gesticulating in a vacuum when he "signed off" from the society into which he was born and refused, as he said, to live in the nineteenth century. He may have had no power to change the course of that century but he did not have to go with it. One might even say that if Pearson is right one may have one's Marxian cake and eat it too. There is a dialectic of matter but an individual may be exempt from it. Perhaps that is enough to make possible what we named, a good many pages back, "the Minimal Man." It is also enough to raise another question. If some are more likely than others to exercise their freedoms then is not sociology unwise to plan society in terms which minimize the importance of those who are most capable of free choices?

To say this is not to say that it is easy to understand how individual freedom and mass enslavement can be possible, or even inevitable—if they are. Obviously we are approaching one of those boundaries beyond which the human mind ceases to function effectively and we have simply to admit that we cannot quite see how what is, can be.

To the hardheaded, to the "realistic" and to the fanatics of common sense whose nostrils will dilate at the first hint of such a suggestion and who will cry in horror "metaphysics," "mystagogery," "obscurantism," etc., one can reply only that science itself is increasingly recognizing the existence of just these boundaries which it finds itself approaching when in pursuit of the merely physical laws governing that matter which, one would suppose, must be far simpler than mind. Here for instance is Dr. James B. Conant, a chemist by profession, summing up the situation as he sees it:

The idea that there could be two diametrically opposed theories as to the nature of heat, of light, or of matter, and that both could be rejected and confirmed as a consequence of experiments would have been considered nonsense to almost all sane people fifty years ago. . . . In regard to light, we can hardly do better than say that light is in a sense both undulatory and corpuscular. In regard to matter, we have already seen that here too a certain ambiguity has entered in. . . . The physicist has learned to live with a paradox that once seemed intolerable. . . . It might be better to say that he has discovered how general is the paradox and by what mathematical manipulations of experimental data he can get forward with all manner of undertakings because of the paradox.

Dr. Conant then goes on with a quotation from Professor P. W. Bridgman's *Philosophical Implications of Physics:*

Finally, I come to what it seems to me may well be from the long range point of view the most revolutionary of the insights to be derived from our recent experiences in physics, more revolutionary than the insights afforded by the discoveries of Galileo and Newton, or of Darwin. This is the insight that it is impossible to transcend the human reference point.

The new insight comes from a realization that the structure of nature may eventually be such that our processes of thought do not correspond to it sufficiently to permit us to think about it at all. We have already had an intimation of this in the behavior of very small things in the quantum domain. . . . There can be no difference of opinion with regard to the dilemma that now confronts us in the direction of the very small. We are now approaching a bound beyond which we are forever stopped from pushing our inquiries, not by the construction of the world, but by the construction of ourselves. . . . We are confronted with something truly ineffable. We have reached the limit of the vision of the great pioneers of science, the vision, namely, that we live in a sympathetic world, in that it is comprehensible to our minds.

By comparisons with pronouncements like these of Conant and Bridgman such an obiter dictum as Sir James

Jean's "the physicist can warn the philosopher that no *intelligible* interpretation of the workings of nature is to be pected" may seem mild.

But it is another straw in a wind which is blowing steadily. Already in the nineteenth century Karl Pearson was saying, "The notion of matter is found to be equally obscure whether we seek for definition in the writings of physicists or of 'common sense' philosophers." In 1940 A. K. Bushkovitch was writing in the periodical *Philosophy of Science*: "Atoms, electrons, and electromagnetic waves are concepts (not to say fictions) invented for the purpose of describing the results of experiments, and of correlating them with each other. An experiment, however, is an operation in which instruments play fully as important a role as the material which is investigated; in fact it cannot be performed and is unthinkable without the instruments. We should no longer talk of understanding the secrets of the universe and learning the ultimate structure of matter." As late as 1953, Einstein—despite his reluctance to accept as readily as many other scientists the concept of indeterminancy as fundamental for physics—had this to say to an interviewer from the Los Angeles *Times* who was questioning him about the deductions concerning human behavior to be drawn from physics: "Man has very little insight into what is going on within himself. Physics has often seduced the biologist into interpreting biological phenomena too primitively."

Those who are appalled by the prospect of living in a universe which, for the first time in several centuries, has ceased to seem comprehensible may be somewhat reassured by the reminder that it is only the novelty of the modern instances which is disturbing and that they have all along been living with other irresolvable paradoxes which did not trouble them simply because they had been for so long accepted.

To the human mind it seems, for example, that both space and time must be either finite or infinite. Yet it is quite impossible for that same mind to see how they can be either. We cannot possibly imagine a time before time existed or a time when it shall have ceased to be. Neither can we imagine either an infinite past or an infinite future. We cannot conceive a space beyond which there is nothing—not even more emptiness. But neither can we conceive the boundless. To say, in the new fashion, that space is curved may solve mathematical difficulties but it presents no picture which we can form. Beside those two ancient paradoxes the paradox of light which is both corpuscular and undulatory, or even the paradox of a human will which is free yet seems bound to obey some statistical law, is relatively easy to accept. And if the last gives us back our minimal human capacities it ought to be welcomed, not feared.

In order to believe in some useful way that we have some power over ourselves, that we can make some choices, and can either recognize or create some values, it is not necessary to solve with absolute finality the metaphysical problem of the freedom of the will any more than it is necessary to solve the paradoxes of time and space in order to live in both. What is necessary is simply to recognize the fact that belief in some sort of autonomy is not incompatible with what is actually known about the behavior of either animate or inanimate matter.

If the meaning of statistical averages is as elusive as so great an authority on statistics as Pearson admits it to be, then the strongest argument in favor of the validity of the whole deterministic Science of Man disappears. The trap has been sprung and we are not caught in it. Perhaps Humanity with a capital "H" is; perhaps you and I are not.

8

THE ABACUS·AND THE BRAIN

THE statement that man behaves like a machine and that therefore he is one, involves two propositions which many physiologists as well as many psychologists appear to regard as demonstrated. It would seem unreasonable to ask that they clinch the argument by proving its obverse; that they conclude the demonstration by making a machine which behaves like a man. No one would really issue so unfair a challenge but many believe that it has been met already. "I think, therefore I am." The electronic calculator thinks, therefore it *is*. Is what? Is a man. Or at least the most important part of him, namely a brain.

Now to understand just what this means and why the argument is dubious, we should really go back as far as the abacus, though to most of us this ingenious device is only a harmless toy of wire and beads. Sometimes our Chinese laundryman plays with it for a few seconds before announcing, "Two dollars and thirty-five cents." We then go our way unaware of danger.

Nobody seems to know who invented this prophetic gadget but whoever did started more than he knew. Arabic numerals came later into Europe and at first they seemed to relegate the abacus to the past. But it was only biding its time. About three hundred years ago John Napier with his "bones" taught the abacus how to be logarithmic instead of merely arithmetical and thus gave to the engineer the slide rule which can multiply or extract square roots faster than he can. Ever since then the human brain has been competing less and less successfully with the machine in the matter of calculation.

When Marconi or De Forest—it was long a vexed question which—invented the grid radio tube, he had no idea that it would be able to figure. Neither, for that matter, did whoever invented the wheeled vehicle have any idea of using it to make pottery, though the anthropologists now tell us that the potter's wheel comes into every culture only after the cart. In other words, most fundamentally new gadgets turn out to be usable in fantastically disparate ways, and the man who made radio practical hit upon a device scarcely less adaptable than the wheel, the wedge or the lever. As everyone knows, contraptions which look rather like huge radios are now solving in minutes, or at most in weeks, problems either totally unsolvable by the human brain or so laborious that an individual would spend a large part of his lifetime with pencil, paper, and slide rule if he tried to work them out.

As is usual when something like this comes along, the result is to make mechanists very happy and the rest of us

uncomfortable. The abacus and the slide rule were merely
tools. Man made them. They were a credit to his ingenuity. They proved how smart *he* was, not how smart *they*
were; and nobody thought of them as having any significance or even any existence apart from him. But these electronic calculators are, we are now told, something quite different. They do not have the limitations which we commonly associate with mechanical devices because electricity
has endowed them with a kind of life. We are assured
that they have memories or, as the followers of Korzybski
would say, that they are the first inorganic thing which is
capable of "time binding." Some people go even so far as
to say that they can exercise judgment, that they think for
themselves. In the opinion of their most ardent admirers
they are less like a machine and more like a human brain
than anything man has ever succeeded in making before.

The poor deluded chemists have been working for a
long time learning to synthesize the amino acids in the
hope that these would lead to synthetic protein and that,
in turn, to synthetic protoplasm. But suppose that at last
they did succeed. What would they have? An amoeba at
best. Your engineer, on the other hand, brushes aside all
nonsense about the mysterious nature of life and, firm in
his conviction that all is mechanical, creates at one fell
swoop life's highest manifestation, namely, thought.

So at least some of them are telling us and we are ill
equipped to argue with them. The equations with which
they juggle may seem like mumbo jumbo to us but they
have proved in many ways that they are not. Mr. Ein-

F

stein writes "$E = MC^2$" and (after a few merely technological intermediary steps) Hiroshima goes up in smoke.
Obviously these mathematicians know what they are talking about and if they tell us that machines are now thinking—just like men only better—perhaps we should marvel
and keep silent.

There is, however, a good deal at stake and it is hard
not to protest a little, not to hope that at least the metaphysical conclusions of some mathematicians and engineers may not be incontrovertible. It is bad enough to be
caught up in a world which whizzes and bangs; bad
enough to be, ultimately, not merely blown up but disinte-
grated. That, however, we are beginning to get used to.
Must we also accept the conviction, not only that we are
victims of the machine, but also that we are merely machines ourselves? If, as is obvious, contraptions are becoming more and more manlike, does it necessarily follow that
man must be assumed to be no more than a contraption
himself?

According to the mechanists, the electronic calculator
is the best new evidence for their side in a long, long time.
So far as I am aware, no one has yet claimed that a calculator can have children, and the power of self-reproduction
has long been on the biologist's list of the criteria for life.
But biologists and engineers do not always see eye to eye,
and the engineer would no doubt be eager to maintain
that if a machine can think, that alone is sufficient to prove
his point—namely that the so-called higher faculties of

man are the result of the operation of physical forces and that the brain is, at most, no more different from a man-made machine than, say, the man-made electronic "valve" is different from the valve we turn on and off at our steam radiator.

You can't see the wheels go round in the brain; but neither can you turn off an electronic valve by hand, though it is a mechanical device nonetheless. The calculator can remember and it can think. The first of these may be one of the lower capacities of the mind, but the second is, by common consent, the highest. Some, indeed, say that among all living things only man and, perhaps, the ape is capable of it. And if that is true, then the calculator is very far up the evolutionary scale, perhaps farther up than man himself. At least it can think better along certain lines than he can.

Unfortunately for those of us who would like to resist this conclusion, it has been prepared for by the whole tendency of thought on such subjects during the last three hundred years. No one can deny that the study of the human body as a machine has been extremely fruitful of results, while theology and metaphysics have often seemed merely to march round and round in their familiar circles. The study of animal and of human *behavior* has led to apparently stable conclusions, while speculations about the soul, or even the mental processes, seemed to get nowhere.

The psychologist, even though he was not clearly a mechanist by conviction, found it more and more advisable to concentrate his attention on instincts and conditioned reflexes. By consequence, we all fell into the habit of assuming that sooner or later all rational need for the consideration of anything else would vanish. What mechanism could not explain was assumed to be a mere residuum growing smaller and smaller. If the body is mostly a machine, then, it seemed, it is probably entirely a machine. And because we had been long prepared, most people were probably relieved to be told that the last objection to mechanism had been removed. Hitherto machines couldn't think. But my new calculator, says the engineer, can. *Quod erat* (for a long time) *demonstrandum*.

If we do not want to accept this demonstration, then it is evident that we cannot resist merely the last steps in the argument, but will have to go a long way back and begin to resist certain premises, long implicit and sometimes concealed. Again we shall have to point out that the very methods which scientists have chosen to use have prejudiced the conclusions; that to observe human or animal behavior *as though* it were merely mechanical, is inevitably to make it seem so; that to begin with the proposition "We cannot conveniently deal with consciousness and therefore we are justified in disregarding it," is simply to invite the confusions which have, in actual fact, arisen. It is to assume that what a given method finds intractable simply does not exist.

Obviously, then, we have to begin by telling the mechanist that, however inconvenient he may find our insistence, we simply will not permit him to disregard any of the facts; not *any* of the facts and, especially, not so tremendous a fact as the fact of consciousness. Descartes, we shall say, was right. That we think—or rather that we are aware—is, of all things, the one which we know most directly and incontrovertibly. It may be a difficult fact to deal with but it is primary. Consciousness is the one thing which incontrovertibly *is,* and if there is one thing which we cannot afford to leave out of consideration it is that. To refuse to concern ourselves with it is to make the most monstrous error that could possibly be made.

Certainly, then, we have a right to ask whether the electronic calculator is conscious. "Does it," we may also ask, "have ideas about itself?" Does it, for example, "believe" that mechanistic theories of life are "true"? These are some of the most important things that the human brain is capable of. No doubt some of the machine's admirers will scornfully reply that we can't prove that it doesn't. But that is hardly enough. If we are going to accept a conclusion so momentous as the conclusion that there is no important difference between us and a circuit of electronic tubes, then we may reasonably ask for more than merely negative evidence. The theory that consciousness is only an epiphenomenon is a theory not a fact. We have a right to say that awareness is the most important as well as the most obvious fact about us. Nothing which is not aware of itself is anything like what we are. It has not been proved that we are machines until it has been proved that a machine can, to begin with—and it is only to begin with—say to itself, *"Cogito ergo sum."* If we are going to deal in mere guesses or probabilities, then some of us may guess that what goes on in a brain is not identical with what goes on in an electronic circuit.

If there was no more to be said than this, it would still be worth saying. To some extent the air would be cleared and we would know where we stand. Those to whom a man is, first of all, a mere figuring machine, would be clearly separated from those to whom consciousness is the essential condition of all those activities which define the human being. But there is more to be said, and there are conclusions to be drawn.

Let us remember that when Diogenes exhibited a plucked hen in the market place and called it "Plato's Man," no one supposed that he meant what he said. He was making it obvious to the meanest intelligence that "a two-legged animal without feathers" is an inadequate definition of man. Similarly when the mechanists exhibit a calculating machine as a contraption whose operations are essentially human, what we ought to conclude is precisely what the ancients concluded from Diogenes' demonstration. Obviously the mechanist's definition of the human being is as inadequate as Plato's definition of man. What he has done is not to prove his point but simply to achieve a glorious *reductio ad absurdum*. What we ought to do is to laugh first, and then to re-examine, not merely the definition so comically exposed, but also the whole long series of dubious assumptions and faulty methods which have led to so preposterous a conclusion. Only at the end of a long series of missteps could anyone be brought to the point where he would be compelled to entertain, even for the purpose of refuting it, the proposition that either a plucked hen or a calculating machine is the same thing as a man.

Moreover definitions are, in this case, extremely important because we tend to cherish and to cultivate in the human race whatever traits and capacities enter into the definition of man which we, at the moment, accept. And it is evident enough that in recent centuries we have fixed our attention chiefly on those aspects of the human being which most resemble, rather than those which least resemble, what a machine is capable of. Not only have we thought of man chiefly in terms of his anatomy, his instincts and his conditioned reflexes, but we have also talked as though the fact that he had an anatomy and had instincts was sufficient proof that the sum of these things was the whole of him.

Even when we have gone beyond anatomy and reflexes to consider his mind, even when we have stopped short of the conviction that this mind was merely a refined manifestation of his ability to acquire habits and become conditioned, we have, nevertheless, tended to consider important chiefly the planning and the calculating powers of this mind. "Man," we have said, "is capable of reason"; not, as we might have said, "capable of hope," or of "doubt," or of "delight"—though all these capacities are certainly as important to him in his experience of living as reason; especially when "reason" means no more than the ability to scheme successfully.

167

In "mental tests," those most characteristically limited manifestations of our concept of the criteria appropriate to the judgment of the human mind, the stress is chiefly upon the ability to analyze and to scheme, so that we put into the category of the most superior men those most likely to scheme successfully and we usually exhibit not the slightest concern over the question whether these "most superior" men are capable, to even an average extent, of the awarenesses, the emotions or the mental reactions which make men attractive, either to themselves or to others. And so, just as the economists have given us the ideal economic man who does nothing but produce and consume, so the mental testers have given us the ideal intelligent man who does nothing except scheme. Between them they have outlined a utopia in which creatures who are really only very flexible calculating machines do nothing except make goods which they then use up—living to eat and eating to live. For such creatures, living in such a world, most of the forms of consciousness would be not only unnecessary but also a burden. In a sense, therefore, the definition of man assumed by the tester prepares us for that definition of man in terms of which the calculator is human.

If we stop to think, most of us do not really believe that the Economic Man is more than a possibly useful methodological fiction, or that the Superior Man of the mental testers is more than simply the man most likely to succeed at tasks requiring the capacities which the tests do actually measure. The fact nevertheless remains that it is to the

Economic Man and the I. Q. Man that our attention is
directed far more often than on the whole man, who is
something very different from either, something far less
like anything the mechanists seem likely to be able to construct. And that fact has its consequences.

Perhaps it is too soon, perhaps it will always be too
soon, to try to formulate an adequate definition of man.
Perhaps the fact that he is indefinable by his own mind is
an essential fact about him. But we might, at least, consider more frequently than we do those of his characteristics which we have got into the habit of thinking about
very seldom. We might, to begin with, ask concerning the
calculating machine those questions posed earlier, and
then add some more. Is it capable, we might ask, of imagination? Does it have any curiosity? Can it sympathize
with anything? Can it be happy or miserable? Was it
ever known to laugh, or even to show, by any unwonted
flickerings in its tubes, that it considered something amus-
ing? Does it—and this is most important of all—prefer
one thing to another, or does it have its being in a universe
where nothing has value, where all things are indifferent?
Presumably we shall not get answers, though some of us
may think we know what the answers would be if we
could get them. But the real reason for asking is not that.
The real reason is that even to ask is to be reminded how
important is the "Yes" we get if we interrogate, not a machine, but a fellow creature; how defective, therefore, is
that so called Science of Man which never really asks the

F*

questions at all and thus proves itself to be, not the Science of Man, but only the Science-of-What-Man-Would-Be-If-He-Were-Not-a-Man-But-a-Machine.

In any event, to ask the questions either of the machine or of ourselves is to take the first step back in the direction of that crossroads, passed perhaps three centuries ago, when we first began to diverge from the path of Wisdom into the path of Inadequate Knowledge. If we retrace our course, we shall be surprised to discover how much we have tended to forget about ourselves, how little we have studied, or even considered, the most remarkable of our capacities. We may even conclude that the ability to figure or to scheme is so far from being our only unique ability that it is not even the most important one—as indeed the possibility of making a machine which can do it for us sufficiently indicates. Perhaps man is not, first of all, a Reasoning Animal; perhaps something else that he does with his mind is even more obviously unique than reasoning. But what, then, shall we call this other thing; what is it that it is hardest to imagine a machine's doing for us?

We might, I suppose, call it "wanting." Certainly even the stupidest man is capable of desiring something, and the cleverest of machines, no matter how brilliantly it may solve differential equations, is not. But the word "wanting" has a more refined and subtler cousin called "preference," which might do better. Man is an animal who not only wants something tangible but is capable also, even among things as insubstantial as ideas or beliefs, of *pre-*

THE ABACUS AND THE BRAIN

ferring one thing to another. And when one has said that, one has arrived at the conventional terminology of metaphysics: Man has a Sense of Values. Other animals may or may not be capable of something out of which the Sense of Values develops. But a machine certainly is not. And there is the grandest of all the differences.

When we think without reference to any preferences or "values" we think like a machine. That means also thinking without reference to joy, or laughter, or love. Very often nowadays we are urged by certain sociologists, political propagandists, and even anthropologists to do just that although they prefer to call it "thinking with detachment." But the thing from which we are asked to detach ourselves is, nevertheless, the state of being human, and the result of such thinking would be a world fit for machines, not for men.

Perhaps, then, those wonderful electronic calculators are not, after all, anything like our brains. Perhaps the best of them is only a super-abacus and therefore a triumph of human ingenuity but, no more than the laundryman's convenient device, a real challenge to the human being's uniqueness. To ask which it is—gadget or brain—is at least no academic question.

To answer one way is to take what is perhaps the final step, not merely in the acceptance of mechanism as a philosophical doctrine, but in the direction of a civilization in which men will become more and more machinelike. To answer the other way is to choose instead the working conviction that man, as he was and as he can be, is neither the Economic Man nor the I. Q. Man but "The Animal Which Can Prefer." It is to believe that the most stupendous of his inventions was not the wheel, or the wedge, or the lever, but the values by which he has lived, and that the ability to act on, for example, the assumption that loyalty is better than treachery even when both seem to give a practical answer to a given problem, is more significant than any other ability he has ever manifested. It is also to believe that, in the future as in the past, what becomes of him will depend less on what machines he invents or what governments are imposed upon him than on what values he creates.

Distrust of our mechanical age, fear that men will be destroyed by the engines which he has devised, is so widespread today that it has developed its own cant. But it often happens that men's fate overtakes them in the one way they had not sufficiently feared, and it may be that if we are to be destroyed by the machine it will not be in quite the manner we have been fearfully envisaging. Perhaps we are in no greater danger of being blown up by the atom bomb than we are of being destroyed by a wrong understanding of the abacus.

9

THE OLD-FASHIONED SCIENCE OF MAN

IN THE course of this discussion reference has been made more than once to the support given by recent science to those who find a paradoxical universe less difficult to believe in than the supposedly understandable one which mechanists undertake to picture. To us it seems that thought, consciousness and the power to choose are realities no matter how difficult they are to reconcile with those other realities which the mechanists stress, and we can say in our defense that both the physicist and the physiologist are now inclined to make the same choice we make when faced with the same difficulty. To them also it seems that they must either reject some of their data or admit that they cannot understand how some of it can be reconciled with the rest. And they also have decided to accept the data which they cannot wholly understand.

What this means is that the mysterious or the incomprehensible is again being recognized by the very sciences which were once supposed to be the implacable enemies of all unsolvable mysteries. And what this seems to mean in turn is that we are now on the point of entering upon a new phase of human thought at least as radically new as any we ever entered before. We had become accustomed to speak of ancient, of medieval, and of "modern" views of the universe and also to assume that the modern had now been established as somehow permanent. But if those physicists are right who remark quite casually that the revolution which the last few years has witnessed in their science is at least as fundamental as the revolution which took place in the sixteenth and seventeenth centuries when the "modern" view assumed definite shape, then the time may be approaching when "modern" will have to mean not the world view of the Newtonian but something quite different, and we shall have to find a new adjective to distinguish the first "scientific world view" from that which has taken its place.

Moreover, and what is perhaps not really suprising, the new "modern view" turns out to be, in at least one respect, more like the medieval than it is like that which immediately preceded it. It recognizes that the human mind is incapable of understanding the universe in quite the sense that nineteenth-century science believed it was on the point of understanding it.

Since the possibilicy that the revolution may be fully accomplished in time to save us from certain consequences of mechanistic hypotheses is one of the chief themes of this book, it may be worth while to examine more closely than we have so far done some of the things that the revolution implies and some of the ways in which the most modern view of the universe resembles—as well as some in which it differs from—that accepted by those who lived before the first great age of science opened. To do so will mean to think for a few minutes, first about what the contemporaries of Newton had to say to those who were still living in Dante's world, and then what the new physicist has to say to those of our contemporaries who are still living in Newton's.

Let us begin by remembering that at the center of Dante's conception of the visible world there was an accepted mystery. The stars in their courses moved in the paths which God had ordained, and this visible world was held together by something called "Love." But there was no attempt to understand the laws in accordance with which this Love operated except in the most general terms —no attempt, for example, to ask in accordance with what law love moved one celestial sphere at one speed and another at another. Perhaps just because Dante's contemporaries felt so sure that they knew the answer to the question "why" the universe existed, they never asked very persistently the question "how" or "in what fashion."

Newton substituted the technical word "gravity" for the frankly mysterious word "love," and he also went on to assure us that the farthest reaches of the universe operate in accordance with the same ascertainable laws that operate upon an apple or, as later philosophers preferred to put it, upon a billiard ball. Though Newton piously assumed that God does, nevertheless, still exist somewhere, he seemed to go a long way toward depriving Him of a continuing function.

What he told us was that in the whole vast extent of the visible universe there is nothing which is not essentially like our own back yard. Let us accept—as we all do—the simple fact that an apple falls. Let us then learn—as we can—the laws which govern the way in which it falls. Once we have done that, there is nothing within the range of our eyes, our telescopes, or even of our imagination that is not explicable by an extension of simple, pragmatic, common sense. There are no mysteries and no paradoxes, at least so far as the *way* in which the tangible universe behaves. So far as it is concerned we know perfectly well what to expect. The heavens are not going to fall unless and until God suddenly and willingly intervenes to blow a last trump. Until then we can say that $S = \frac{1}{2}gt^2$ and that $\frac{ds}{dt} = gt$. That is all there is to it.

This Newtonian universe may be a little bit dull, but at least there is nothing about it to provoke anxiety until the day of the last trump. Even now most people instinctively try to live in it. The general temper which it expresses is the one to which they try to cling, and it is only upon the periphery of their consciousnesses, upon that periphery where anxieties are generated, that they permit themselves to be somewhat vaguely aware of what the newer science in which they profess also to believe has done to this dully uniform and regular universe.

To take a single instance, we are being told by at least certain of Newton's successors that instead of living in an infinitely extended back yard, even the back yard is not at all what it seems; that so far as the universe as a whole is concerned we do not know how it is operating or where it is going; that common sense is wholly inadequate to comprehend it, and that, in so far as one can guess, we are actually somewhere in a sort of soap bubble which is expanding at an inconceivable but ever increasing rate and, for all we know, may burst. Obviously this universe seems a great deal less dependable, a great deal more an occasion for a certain amount of anxiety, than Newton's was. It is also a great deal more mysterious and a great deal more repugnant to common sense than even Dante's. We seem, in other words, to have come a full circle—out of what we used to call the darkness of ignorance into the light of common day, and then back again into the incomprehensible.

When what we still carelessly call the "modern" world view began to take shape in the seventeenth century, it was the result of a revolt of common sense against everything that was repugnant to it. It was a declaration of faith in the senses as opposed to the speculative mind and in the visible world as opposed to the unseen. Today, however, we are beginning to admit that common sense has been defeated again. Once more we live in a universe which is not at all what it seems, either to the senses or to common sense. Even the external world which we think we see does not exist in the form in which it is present to us. What we think we see with our eyes or touch with our hands seems to us to exist in that form only because our senses give us a false, or at least a grossly inaccurate, report of it; and hence even the world of matter as we think we perceive it is as illusory as it was ever said by the mystics to be.

To them the world was all Spirit. By us it is now said to be all Energy. But to Animal Faith, to everyday experience, to that common sense to which the first modern scientists appealed, the one is as essentially meaningless as the other, and a Bacon, a Hobbes or, for that matter, a Lucretius would have seen little to choose between them. The doctrine of the Trinity was once thought to be hard to swallow. How, asked rationalists, can what is Three be also One? But how, for that matter, can time curve back upon itself or the finite universe be a sphere beyond whose boundaries there is not even nothingness—unless perhaps there are other finite universes. Can anyone maintain that the mysteries of the Trinity are any more mysterious than curving space? What can any modern physicist do except echo the phrase commonly attributed in garbled form to Tertullian and once regarded as the very ecstasy of unreason: "I believe because it is impossible"?

Moreover, the internal world as it is described by the "new psychology" is as contrary to our own conscious experience as is the external world described by the physicists. We are told, to begin with, that consciousness is only a small part, often a self-deceiving part, of our total selves.

Both our thoughts and our actions are usually determined by mental processes of which we are unaware, and if it is at all possible for us to obey the classical injunction, "Know thyself," it is certainly not possible by any sort of mere self-examination.

When a medieval man committed a crime he might very well be in doubt why he did so. So far as what we should call his conscious mind was concerned, it may have seemed to him that he simply consented to wickedness. But he thought he knew, as many of us again think we know, that one is aware of only a very small part of what goes on in himself, that we are often under the domination of what the medieval man called "spiritual forces" and we call "the unconsciousness." In either case certain forces of which he or we can have no conscious knowledge were at work. To him there was always the possibility that a demon had tempted him; to us there is always the possibility—some would say the certainty—that some conditioning had made it inevitable that we should come to what appears to us as simply an evil decision.

It must be remembered moreover that the proofs offered by theologians on the one hand, and by social psychologists on the other, of the truths of their premises are essentially similar and come down in the end to pragmatic demonstrations addressed, as the theories are not, to common sense. Thus social psychologists offer to demonstrate that the criminal has been conditioned; that slums breed crime; and that bad boys become good boys when provided with a proper environment. In the Middle Ages, on the contrary, it seemed, and probably was equally evident, that conversion to Christianity often produced reform and that a man who was persuaded to repent often led a godly life henceforth. Certainly the saints were often genuinely saintly. It would be difficult to prove that modern education has ever produced superior prodigies of heroism and selflessness. But in either case only inference can assign a cause since in both cases the cause is said to lie outside the realm of direct self-knowledge.

The question at issue is not whether one theory is truer than the other. It is quite possible that the unconsciousness does exist and that demons do not. But the fact remains that the medieval mind accepted and the present-day mind again accepts a physical world which is not what it seems and a mental world which is dominated by forces of which is has no conscious awareness. These physical and mental worlds are more alike than the one is like the physical world of Newton or the other like the mental world of Hobbes, Locke, or even Hume. Willy-nilly we have become mystagogues again.

On the whole we are probably quite right to assume that the unconsciousness does exist. But it is a curious fact that Freud should remain in many of his attitudes so much a child of the Enlightenment despite that fact that he has based everything on a concept which would have seemed to the Enlightenment itself as dubious as, for instance, Conscience or the Voice of God. Freud himself, and even more conspicuously his more positivistic followers, dismiss with bluff contempt such concepts as "God," the "Soul," and the "Sense of Sin." In a manner strongly suggestive of the Enlightenment, they reinterpret all these as explicable divagations of the understandable processes of the mind. They will have nothing to do with the ineffable and the mysterious—or rather nothing to do with mysteries which are not new mysteries. Yet the truth is, of course, that the unconsciousness is as purely hypothetical as the Soul and that certain of Freud's other key concepts—notably that of the Censor—are obviously devoid of any objectively demonstrable correlatives and that they are sometimes admitted, even by those who employ them, to be no more than metaphors serving to recognize the existence of something whose nature and mode of operations are both uncomprehended. No anatomist can tell us in neurological terms how the Censor operates.

Once Freudianism was accepted, it put an end to the whole nineteenth-century dream of making the science of the mind a physical or physiological science. Freud himself stopped looking in the physical brain for the evidence or the cause of mental phenomena. To some extent he tried to conceal the real nature of what he was doing by calling the disorders "functional"; but that is largely a matter of vocabulary. What he really did was to reintroduce the concept of the Soul and that fact cannot be concealed by using only the Greek for it and calling it always the Psyche. To the old jibe of the materialist who said that he had never been able to find a soul in his test tube might be added a new one: "I have never been able to find a Censor there either."

Clerk-Maxwell's famous joke about his inability to explain what really happens during the interchange of two gases at different temperatures except on the assumption of a trap door operated by a demon who decides to exclude certain molecules while allowing others to pass, has turned out to be no joke. Demons of one kind or another have again become, as in the Middle Ages they were, indispensable in all kinds of sciences, from physics, which used to be no more than simple mechanics, to psychology which some of its earlier students tried to make no more than a matter of physiology. As William James was already insisting more than a generation ago, the Newtonian billiard-ball universe no longer affords a tenable description of even mechanical processes. Yet both the average man and the thinking man try desperately to hold onto it, and refuse to accept the full consequences of the fact that the whole universe has again become a paradox.

During the Enlightenment physics set itself up as the avowed enemy of metaphysics. It came to be asserted finally that if we would only cease to bother about the "why" and confine ourselves exclusively to the question "how," there would no longer be any permanently disputable subjects. To this day the positivist philosophers try to dispose of the traditional problems of philosophy by declaring that they are devoid of meaning and do not need to be asked. But one obvious result of the "new" physics and the "new" psychology has been to reintroduce them—often in almost identical form—and to make them crucial in any attempt to understand even the "how." Thus if the terms

"Psyche" and "unconsciousness" are more than metaphors and therefore really science rather than mere poetry, they raise again the whole problem of the relation between body and mind, thought and chemistry.

No metaphysical question is more traditional, more elusive, or more thorny. None presents more persistently that evidence of its genuineness which consists in the fact that it arises no matter on what level of subtlety one operates. To the naïve it used to be simply the question of how the Soul got into the body, or what intercourse the one had with the other, and in what form the one persisted after the other had ceased to function. But the problem continued to plague the subtlest and most abstract analysis when it reappeared in the form of the question what sort of traffic "thought" could have with "matter"; how the *Idea* of an object could be produced by the object itself.

The Idea is self-evident to the mind which is aware of it; the material object is merely inferred from the presence of the Idea. But the two realities—if indeed the second is assumed to be real at all—are qualitatively and absolutely distinct; seem to have their being in discontinuous realms. And it was this fact which drove Berkeley to the famous paradox which has often been dismissed but never logically resolved. For Berkeley did not deny that matter exists. What he did maintain was that *if* matter existed *merely* as matter, we could not possibly be aware of it, since the "ideas" which we have of matter are obviously not material and cannot be part of it. If, therefore, these ideas do arise out of and do correspond to the thing called matter, then matter itself must be dual. It must, in accord with the Platonic notion, be ideal as well as material and the only contact which our minds can have with it must be via that ideal aspect which corresponds to our own idea.

Now the most curious and most important fact is that while the "new" psychology calls renewed attention to the body-mind problem, the "new" physics suggests a different approach to that problem by its own novel solution of what looks like an analogous problem. To common sense and to classical physics alike the fundamentally different realities called Matter and Energy seems as absolutely different in their nature and substance as Mind and Body, or Mind and Matter. Every elementary textbook used to begin by defining the two as ultimates, each to be accepted without further analysis and impossible in any way to equate. That both exist and that both are primary is insisted on with the same lack of qualification that one would expect to find in the case of Mind or Soul and Matter as defined in the first paragraph of a popular treatise on religion.

The question how Energy or even Force could operate upon Matter involved a metaphysical question closely analogous to that of the Mind-Matter question. Long before the almost apocalyptic proclamation of Einstein's conversion formula the concept of Gravity had troubled the thoughtful and come to seem actually as incomprehensible as Dante's Love and superior to it as an explanation of what moves the material masses of the universe only because it could be mathematically formulated, not at all because it seemed to mean any more. Here was a Force—the most all-pervasive of all Forces—and yet one which not only affected the material without being itself material but was, in other ways, even more mysterious than other forces because it was omnipresent, invariable, and not to be modified. Indeed, many began to suspect that Gravity was not a Force at all, that the fact that we had to call on it to explain the universe indicated some radical error in our conception of the real universe in which Gravity might be not a separate thing but something inherent in the nature of Matter existing in space-time.

But the possible solution of the special problem of Gravity seems relatively quite unimportant by comparison with the solution of the whole Matter-Energy problem. The formula $E = MC^2$ (now repeated in many popular discussions almost as a kind of incantation) actually does have implications sensational beyond those of any other formula whatsoever. What it says is that the only two supposedly primary, discontinuous, fundamentally different realities of the physical universe are not discontinuous or fundamentally different at all, that instead of being qualitatively different they are actually quantitatively convertible. Moreover, the operation of the atom bomb is said to give empirical evidence of the truth of the revolutionary pronouncement. Thus the writing of the formula followed by the practical experiment makes the whole situation very much like the one which might arise if it were suddenly announced that so much body was the equivalent of so much mind, or so much Matter the equivalent of so much Idea, and if the possibility of the conversion of one into the other were then demonstrated by the disappearance of part of an object when some mind became aware of it.

Inevitably a new possibility now suggests itself. Perhaps the positivists who argue that we ask meaningless questions are right in a way they did not suspect. Perhaps the questions how mind can occupy a body or how a force can operate upon matter are meaningless questions because they are based on the false assumption that in both cases two different kinds of reality are involved. Perhaps the materialist and the idealist, the mechanist and the vitalist are not disputing about anything which is real. What is the use of declaring that Man is a Machine or that Man is a Spirit; that thought is a chemical process in the brain, or that thought cannot be reduced to physical processes; what is the meaning of such disputes if the distinction between the material and the nonmaterial is as unreal as the distinction between matter and energy.

If this is not a universe composed of Matter *and* Energy but of Matter-Energy why should it be assumed that it must remain, nevertheless, one which is either Material or Ideal? To suppose that it may, on the contrary, be both; that what we call "matter" is one manifestation of "thought," is no more repugnant to common sense or experience than the declaration that matter and energy are different manifestations of the same thing. It is ridiculous for anyone to say that he is a materialist or a vitalist when we cannot know what the distinction between the two is unless we are sure, as now we are not, what matter may be capable of.

That the so-called Galileo-Newton revolution was not a revolution at all in the same sense that the Einsteinian revolution genuinely is, can be easily illustrated by a comparison of a formulation typical of each. Such a formulation will show very well how the one stayed within the bonds of common sense and the other did not.

$S = \frac{1}{2}gt^2$ describes the way in which a falling body—for instance the legendary apple of Newton's tree—falls. It states that the distance which it falls in a given time is equal to one half the square of the number of seconds it has been falling, multiplied by a number "g" which varies slightly at different points on the earth. Everyone who had ever used his senses to observe the phenomenon knew that such a body fell faster and faster the longer it fell. All that this formula does is to describe more accurately, by reducing to quantitative terms, what experience had taught. To extend it as Newton did to the whole solar system involves nothing paradoxical. All you have to do is to state that wherever in the universe two bodies are falling toward one another they do so in a manner described by the same law—"g" in every case being taken to be a constant defined by the mass of one body in relation to the mass of the other and by the distance between them. The only effect of this announcement is to make the universe seem more regular, more uniform, and more dependable than it was previously known to be. It is not at all to violate the common sense but rather to confirm it.

On the other hand, to say with Einstein that $E = MC^2$ is to say something entirely different in its effect. To assert that matter can be turned into energy, that a given mass is equivalent to an amount of energy equal to that mass multiplied by (of all things!) the square of the speed of light, is to fly in the face of all ordinary experience. In Newton's case the novelty consisted chiefly in reducing the thing to exact measurement. In Einstein's case the startling fact is not the statement how much matter is equivalent to how much energy but simply the assumption that the two are somehow equivalent—which is an assumption common sense would never have made.

To be told that on the deserts of New Mexico and in the air above Japan certain lumps of matter simply ceased to be, is to be told something which common sense—confirmed by all science which could claim to be merely an extension of common sense—would call impossible nonsense. To be told further that the process is no doubt reversible, that matter may disappear and then be created again, is to be compelled to reconsider our most fundamental assumptions concerning the nature of reality. What was once ultimate is ultimate no longer. What we once thought of as the inexplicable and never-to-be-repeated first creation of matter may be taking place every day. Newton told us that the mysterious heavens were as knowable to common sense as our own back yard; Einstein tells us that our own back yard is as mysterious as the heavens were ever supposed to be.

Samuel Johnson was once asked whether he thought that anybody believed the truths of religion *in the same sense* that he believed the facts of everyday life; and Dr. Johnson, profoundly religious though he was, replied with a categorical "No, sir." The incident reminds us that "levels of belief" are very real and that Animal Faith is usually stronger than belief of any other kind. Does anybody, one must therefore ask, believe the truths of the newest science in the same sense that he believes the facts of everyday life? And the answer should be an equally categorical "No."

Probably most of us do not even believe that the sun is ninety million miles away in the same sense we believe that the post office is five blocks from our front door. But our difficulty in believing that is only the difficulty of believing something quantitatively outside our experience rather than contrary to it. Most of us therefore probably do believe it in some sense which may be less than our belief in what Animal Faith consents to, while it is nevertheless stronger than our belief in things like the matter-energy transformation which are not only outside of, but also repugnant to, experience.

Nevertheless the fact remains that the more different levels of belief on which the mind is compelled to operate and the less clear the distinctions between them, the more difficult it becomes for us really to "know our own minds."

And though the scientific age began with the determination to eliminate as far as possible all those levels which could not be reconciled with Animal Faith, it has ended by reintroducing them, so that our position has become more analogous to that of the fifteenth-century man who did not know whether or not he believed in Hell, than it is to that of the nineteenth-century scientific mind which was far more certain of what it genuinely believed and far less given to asserting belief in what it was actually only trying to understand.

Of course no one can be sure that this state of affairs is permanent. Certain of the most ineffable conceptions of mathematical physics, like curved space and spherical time, may someday again be dismissed as impossible fancies. But it is not likely that the back-yard universe will ever be re-established unless civilization and the human mind should devolve to some condition where much that has been discovered and thought is lost.

Moreover, and what is more important for the moment, the probabilities are that at least for some time to come, science is going to be less and less translatable into common-sense terms. It seems reasonable to conclude that the man who wishes to understand the world in which he lives will do well to accept the fact and to stop attempting, as he so often does attempt, to understand more of it in terms of common sense and old-fashioned science than can actually be understood in those terms.

Our inconsistencies are most glaring in such areas as those of politics, sociology and morals, where the methods employed are least clearly defined. There, empirical snap judgments, the prejudices of Animal Faith, and scientific pretensions of some sort, all meet. And the fact that they all do meet there helps explain why these so-called Sciences of Man, even when they are scientific at all, tend to lag so far behind the physical sciences—not only (as is generally admitted) in their results, but also (as is not so generally admitted) in respect to the very premises on which they are founded. It explains why, to put the thing as bluntly as possible, the theories and methods most prevalent among social scientists are mechanistic, deterministic, and materialistic; why they cling so stubbornly to old-fashioned prejudices against admitting the existence of intangibles and unpredictables; why they continue to do so when the actual sciences dealing with a physical world much less complicated than the human world have completely abandoned the attempt to describe or deal with it in any such way. Many physicists have given "free will" back to the atoms, but many sociologists still seem to deny it to the human being.

It is those who profess to describe, predict, and control human behavior that speak with outdated contempt of what they call mystical notions and are prone to deny that there is anything which cannot be accounted for without recourse to any concepts less mechanistic than instinct and conditioning. They insist on treating even the world of consciousness as though it were analogous to that billiard-ball universe which was long ago abandoned by the sciences that deal with "dead" matter, and they would make the Science of Man simpler than physics. They refuse to grant to the individual human being that degree of individuality and unpredictability now granted to the atom and they insist on remaining materialists in a world where matter, as an ultimate persisting reality, has ceased to exist.

That the paradoxes of physics are possibly only provisional is irrelevant. It is true, for instance, that Einstein himself, having done so much to make the universe mysterious, has expressed the conviction—admittedly a pure act of faith and certainly not agreed to by many physicists —that somehow and at sometime the paradox of the atom will be resolved in such a way as to re-establish determinism at least to the extent that energy and matter will be demonstrated to behave in a completely predictable manner. But the important point is that in physics the most useful working hypotheses at this moment seem to be those which freely acknowledge an unpredictable element as well as various other things that would have seemed absurdly paradoxical two generations ago. The suggestion made here is that the Sciences of Man might do well to accept a little more freely than they seem inclined to do the possibility that man himself is at least as mysterious as a lump of uranium.

Despite the large claims which are made, it is not completely self-evident that the most generally accepted methods of these sciences have been entirely successful in, say, the education of the young and the prevention of crime. It has already been pointed out that the crime rate admittedly

rises, and it has already been remarked that we cannot
logically take it for granted that it would have risen still
faster if the methods used to prevent it had been less completely those which the social sciences have recommended.
But leaving aside the debatable question of the extent to
which they have been successful in controlling human
behavior, it seems even more legitimate to question whether their assumptions have contributed to the psychic health
and comfort of the human being who cannot very well
accept their mechanistic implications as valid for others
unless he accepts them as valid for himself also.

When he does so accept them, he finds himself living
in a human society where he must surrender for himself as
well as for his fellows certain rights, privileges, and dig-
nities which, nevertheless, continue to seem real in the
world of his own intimate experience. If the deepest convictions of others are always or even chiefly the results of
their conditioning, so must his be. His sense of right and
wrong, his standard of value must be, like theirs, not convictions won by his own independent mind but the predictable results of the environment in which he has lived.
Even his decision to do or not to do what seems to him
wicked or criminal is not really his decision; and if he
agrees that others can and should be molded and manipu-
lated into convictions as well as into patterns of conduct
which social scientists have agreed to find desirable, he
must himself submit to such moldings and manipulations.
Quite literally his soul is no longer his own.

Moreover, and even if he believes that he is willing to

consent to all this, it will still be as an autonomous individual capable of making his own decisions that he will continue to appear to himself in his own consciousness. And it may very well be that another reason why this age is an Age of Anxiety is to be found in the contradictions inevitably incident to a life in two irreconcilable worlds—the world of intimate experience and that world of abstract convictions in which the validity of intimate experience is categorically denied.

The purpose of this book is to examine certain aspects of the prevailing mood and temper. Inevitably that examination has involved at various points the influence of the assumptions and methods of those social sciences which directly attempt to affect the mood and which also, incidentally and indirectly, influence it still further simply by virtue of the fact that many people have pretty generally accepted certain of their assumptions and approved of their methods. The belief that, for instance, the most important thing about a human being is the fact that he has been "conditioned" may affect a human being more profoundly than any deliberate "conditioning" to which he has been subjected.

For this, as well as for other reasons, it may be that the social sciences would have served mankind better and would have more successfully promoted even that "adjustment" they lay so much store by if they had been as willing as the physicists have shown themselves to admit the unpredictable, intangible and paradoxical aspects of nature and behavior. Their attempts to minimize and disregard the importance of conscious process, to deny the autonomy of the individual mind, to reject as without real significance the hard facts of direct intimate experience, and to insist on regarding consciousness itself as a deluding epiphenomenon, has done more than encourage a split between the two worlds in which moderns try to live. It has also resulted in a theoretical picture of the human universe which is both fantastically complicated and startlingly inadequate: complicated because its attempts to explain away the apparent reality behind such concepts as free will and the ethical sense are necessarily very elaborate; inadequate because the most ambitious mechanical man remains obviously a very incomplete one.

The suggestion is not that we must return to theology, to simple Christian belief, or to anything else. But the suggestion, or rather the insistence, is that the old-fashioned Science of Man is as inadequate to account for man himself as Newtonian physics is inadequate to account for the universe in which man has his physical being. Behind the ancient and possibly quite unsatisfactory concepts of free will, individual responsibility and the validity of value judgments, lie some realities without the recognition of which it is not possible to manage a world in which human beings will be either successful or happy.

The minimum responsibility of the social sciences is to recognize this fact freely and to make some serious attempt to find out what those realities are. They will never help us solve our problems as long as they continue to go on the assumption that whatever is true of a rat is true of a man. Indeed they will not be able to solve them so long as they assume that even a rat is adequately accounted for on the basis of mechanistic premises.

If it should turn out, as it probably will, that they cannot investigate the reality behind the key concepts without reconciling themselves, either permanently or temporarily, to paradoxes not resolvable by common sense, then they had better follow the physicists who have already done just that. There is certainly no reason for assuming that the human being is both simpler and more mechanical than the ultimate particles out of which actual machines are made. If Matter can become Energy, there seems no great difficulty in believing that the physical stuff of the brain may become Mind—in some sense as different from the protoplasm of a cell as the energy released over Japan was different from the matter which disappeared when that energy came into being.

10

THE FUNCTION OF DISCOURSE

To raise doubts and reveal paradoxes has
been, so far, the principal aim of this discourse. Most of
the emphasis has been on what we do not know rather
than on what we do; on the limitations of the human understanding, not on the probability that it has yet, or perhaps ever will, reduce ultimate reality to a comprehensible
unity from which everything paradoxical has been removed.

No pretense is made that the validity of hypotheses other
than the mechanistic has been definitely established. It has
been suggested that some realm of human freedom may
exist, that value judgments may have some ultimate meaning, that thought and preference may be in some way autonomous; but all these propositions remain hypothetical.
At most it has been argued that they cannot be rejected unless we are willing to accept an alternate set of propositions
full of logical difficulties and impossible to reconcile with
primary experience. The physicist who finds himself

forced to admit that many things, each demonstrably true, seem to be inconsistent with one another, and who therefore accepts each separate phenomenon as somehow significant even though he cannot fit them all into any unified scheme, suggests that a similar quasi solution of our difficulties may be the best we can achieve. If light behaves as though it were both undulatory and corpuscular, the paradox is no less difficult to resolve than the paradox of man who seems both free and to some extent predictable by statistical methods. Like the atom he seems both to obey laws and to "hop about."

All the doubts and difficulties do, moreover, justify one positive conclusion. No one who has considered them has a right to say that we are *compelled* by logic or evidence to accept the materialist-determinist credo or even that all of whatever evidence we have is in its favor. Whoever does continue to insist dogmatically on that credo chooses to do so. He prefers that opinion and he wants the kind of society he believes it will produce. He has not any longer an excuse for saying, "I cannot do otherwise."

As a matter of fact, the balance of evidence is less in his favor than it was a generation ago. It seems more reasonable now than it did then to suggest that the whole question be reconsidered; to ask whether it would be worth while, even as an experiment, to act more often on certain assumptions we have tended to dismiss. What was called at the beginning of this discourse "the grand strategy" of recent history might be drastically revised if, for example, we should, for a while, base our private and our public behavior on the premise that freedom is a reality, that value judgments are possible and important, that men are capable of making decisions for themselves.

Socially, such an experiment might ultimately mean less stress on what can be done to our fellow citizens; more on the opportunities given them to do something for themselves—even on our readiness to make some distinction, moral and otherwise, between those who do and those who do not take advantage of the opportunity. Politically it might make possible a clarification of the difference between democratic and totalitarian ideals.

It is certainly because such clarification has never been accomplished that the ideological struggle between the two is at the moment so hopelessly confused and that it often comes down to no more than the rival claims of two political parties concerning what each has accomplished in providing the masses under its control with those "goods" which both define in the same way.

Both are humanistic or at least humanitarian in the narrow sense that both profess to regard what we call the "welfare" of the citizen as the only thing which really counts. Both are clearly distinguishable from political or social philosophies which put something other than human welfare—say the Glory of God, or the glory of the abstract national state—before the happiness and prosperity of the common man. But actually and despite the tendency to speak of democracy and totalitarianism as completely antithetical it is often very difficult to see any very sharp logical distinction between what is often meant by the one or the other; and it is because of this fact that at least a minority of our citizens can be seduced by Communist professions and the claim that communism as a political system has actually achieved the "welfare" which the democracies only profess to want.

The paradox in democratic thinking which makes the confusion possible is precisely the one with which we have all along been concerned. It is inherent in the fact that while we have exalted man's importance by making his "welfare" the measure of all things, we have, at the same time, belittled him by assuming that he is, nevertheless, nothing in himself. If we could say to the Communist, "There is one supremely important respect in which we differ from you. We believe, as you do not, that freedom is real, that choices are possible, and that man can think as well as rationalize," then we would know—as now we often do not—what the meaning of our conflict really is. We could say that the traditional instruments of democratic government—free discussion, the secret ballot, etc.— are not the mere fetishes which Communists sometimes call them, but genuinely important because they furnish a method by which the autonomous desires and preferences of the free individual can influence the course of political history. But we cannot say that now, because too many so-called democrats do not believe anything of the sort, and to them, whether they know it or not, the traditional instruments of democratic government are therefore, in fact, little more than fetishes.

The grand paradox of our society is this: we magnify

man's rights but we minimize his capacities. And it is only in some totalitarian theory that this paradox can be resolved. Sub-men cannot rule themselves. The best government, therefore, can only be one which is *for* but not *by* them. More and more clearly it becomes apparent how absurd it is to talk about a "free society" if that society is to be composed of individuals who cannot possibly be other than what circumstances make them. From what or for what could such individuals be free? Against repressive institutions free men might ultimately rebel, but no institutions can bestow freedom if freedom itself is never more than an illusion. Neither civil nor political liberties can be enjoyed by creatures unable to take advantage of them.

Should social and political effects like those just suggested actually be produced they would, however, probably follow rather than precede a certain refocusing of the individual man's attention and his rediscovery within himself of seeming realities and seeming truths he has got into the habit of disregarding. His own inner life would first be reconstructed, and he would find himself more inclined than he now is to seek in his own consciousness for the meaning of various phenomena which he has been taught to interpret only in the terms of "objective" studies which, because of the very methods they employ, cannot possibly concern themselves with the most vivid and decisive of his experiences. Even if he continued to believe that the world of consciousness represents only one aspect of reality and that another lies outside the reach of that conscious-

G*

ness, he would, nevertheless, still find himself encouraged to take some account of both aspects and thus to have some real knowledge of the two fragments of ultimate reality.

Many intimate experiences are at least as real in their own way as the sense experiences for which the brain is ultimately no less responsible. No sane man ever urged that in our ordinary daily lives we should disregard such sense experiences as irrelevant and acknowledge only the undulating ether and the chemical reactions which are said by physical science to be the significant realities behind vision and taste. Yet the intellectual, moral, and emotional concomitants of behavior are as indisputably real in their own way as the sensations which accompany the impingement of material particles upon the nerve ends in our bodies. We "make decisions" almost as vividly as we see purple or taste garlic. The universe of values, moral and aesthetic, is almost as vividly present as the world of sensation.

Both are part of the universe in which man has his being. The sense of making choices, of entertaining preferences, and of forming resolutions is as real to him as the sensation of color. All the components of the universe of consciousness have, at a minimum, a relation to the "real world" of mere behavior as genuine as any the world of sensation has to the "real world" of physics and chemistry.

To recognize these facts does not mean that we must always or completely disregard the findings of the orthodox sociologist or dismiss the explanations of the psychologist. Their methods and their results may be as legitimate and, in certain situations, as useful as the physicist's investigation of the principles of optics. But it does mean that we should recognize their inadequacy when they claim to represent the only possible approach to a comprehension of total reality. Above all it means that when we deny the more immediately present universe of sensations and of human concepts we lose the ability to manage or even to *live* our own lives in any way meaningful to a human being. It means, to take the simplest and most concrete kind of example, that a human being cannot remain human if, when faced with a problem or aware of a preference, he does not try to reason about the one or examine the implications of the other but simply accepts with a shrug the assumption that society has created the problem and his conditioning determined the preference. One might almost as well give up the whole enterprise of thinking if one never permits oneself to say, "I am convinced of so and so," without adding immediately, "But of course I recognize that it is either certain or at least highly probable that I would not be convinced of anything of the sort had it not happened that my social or individual conditioning had made it inevitable that I should be."

Yet it is actually some such radical distrust of all human reason that is encouraged by the pronouncements sometimes made by men who may not really wish to produce any such effect and may not actually hold deterministic theories in their most extreme form. Consider, for example, the statement made by Professor Leslie White of the Department of Anthropology at the University of

Michigan in the course of an address before a recent meeting of the American Association for the Advancement of Science: "In a realistic, scientific and non-anthropocentric sense, it is the culture that thinks, feels, acts and revolts. It does these things through the medium of human organisms." From the address as a whole it is obvious that Professor White does not deny that individual members of a given society react somewhat differently to the pressures of that culture. But the whole effect of his position is to emphasize uniformity and predictability so strongly that government, education, and moral philosophy are all encouraged to concentrate their attention on the standardized man rather than on even such individuality as is admitted to exist.

Or take the case of the admirable review of an admirable book which appeared in the *Nation* for August 22, 1953. The subject is the evolution of those intellectual and moral convictions which the original settlers of New England brought with them. Says the reviewer, "The old theological and philosophical structure which once had seemed proof against all storms was pretty well smashed. Its materials, warped and hacked out of shape, waited a new builder who could make use of them to construct an intellectual and moral system suited to the new needs and aspirations of Massachusetts."

Taken by itself, there is certainly nothing to object to in this statement. Few would want to deny that "needs and aspirations" have an influence on what either individuals or societies believe. But it is significant of our own habits of thought that it should be taken for granted that the meaning of both philosophy and theology must be explored, primarily if not exclusively, in the light of "needs and aspirations"; that no realistically minded man would think it his first duty to inquire how a philosophy determined what men believed to be their "needs" rather than how "needs" determined the philosophy. Though the reviewer just quoted would perhaps not be willing to state that philosophical convictions are mere epiphenomena phosphorescent on the dialectic of material cultures, that is what he seems to imply.

A few years ago the *New Yorker* magazine published a picture in which a small boy stands face to face with his father who is examining an obviously unsatisfactory report card. "Well, dad," inquires the child, "which do you suppose it is: heredity or environment?" The impasse reached by a civilization which has accepted sociology but rejected the terms in which human life presents itself to the human mind could not be more concisely summarized.

If the sense of making choices and of entertaining preferences, along with all the other components of conscious life, are, like consciousness itself, merely epiphenominal and therefore in some sense illusory, then we are creatures who owe our whole past history, who owe the very state of being human at all, to our extraordinary capacity for being more at home among illusions than among realities, and we are in some curious way epiphenominal ourselves. But if—and it seems at least possible—all of what seem to be human capacities and human traits have somehow either always existed or at some time struggled into being by becoming genuine phenomena in their own right, then a large part of the whole modern effort to achieve what is commonly called an understanding of reality may be in fact an attempt to destroy what has been slowly emerging or slowly coming to be recognized. It may be a deliberate turning away from the most significant realities and a stubborn refusal to recognize them.

In that case, what is commonly called "the fallacy of origins" takes on an added significance. It involves something more than the usually recognized error which we make when we assume, for instance, that patriotism is "nothing but" a determination to profit from the prosperity of our tribe, that honor is "nothing but" a reflex action in accordance with the pattern to which we have been conditioned, or that love is "nothing but" the biological urge to reproduction. Such errors are commonly assumed to be, at most, a failure to distinguish between the parts of a continuous series of essentially similar phenomena. But if the series is actually discontinuous; if, for example, honor becomes at some point something new, something radically different from the conditioned reflex which seems to be all that can be discovered in certain aspects of behavior, then the fallacy is much more monstrous than was supposed and the consequences are far more serious.

Perhaps the time has come to reconsider the whole problem of the cart-and-the-horse to which the Platonic tradition gave one positive answer and modern thought has tended to give, even more dogmatically, an opposite one. Because of the long-fixed habit of our minds it seems to us almost self-evident that the simpler, grosser, most obviously material and most mechanistically explicable manifestations of any phenomenon are the realest and the most fundamental. Even when we admit, for example, that love may manifest itself in a form we can usefully distinguish from simple sexual desire, that honor may evolve into something equally distinguishable from a simple code of class behavior based on class interest, and that, in general, morals are not quite identical with mores, we still usually tend to regard the one as having its origins at least in "nothing but" the other.

The suggestion that the true explanation might begin at the other end; the notion that, for instance, sexual desire might be regarded as the simplest and crudest manifestation of an equally fundamental reality called "love," and that we might, therefore, speak of sexual desire as "nothing but" a manifestation of love—all such suggestions strike us as childish and mythological. Yet on purely a priori grounds the one explanation is no less tenable than the other, and the chief reason why we prefer our usual one is simply the fact that the physical sciences have accepted it as a master key.

Once we try, merely as an experiment, the alternate hypothesis, we discover that everything we have explained to ourselves in one way can be explained in the other. When Freud says that the human need for a trust in God the Father is "nothing but" a projection of the need for an earthly one, a theologian might reply that, on the contrary, the human need to repose trust in the head of a natural family is "nothing but" the analogue, on a lower plane, of his even more fundamental need for that God who is the father of all. Indeed one may go even further and argue that when the materialist begins by assuming the reality of the physical world and concludes, therefore, that consciousness must be somehow the product of it, he is less justified than the idealist who assumes that, since mind is the fundamental reality, then all of what we call the material world must be some sort of projection from consciousness. After all it is consciousness alone of which we have direct evidence; everything else exists only by inference from it.

Perhaps the real truth is that our statement of the cart and horse problem is itself based on a misconception. Perhaps the relationship between mind and matter, as well as the relationship between sex and love, is not as simple as the metaphor suggests or as either Platonic idealism or scientific realism suppose. In medicine the mergence of psychosomatic theories signals the breakdown of simpler concepts of the relation between body and mind in much the same way that the concepts of the new physics signalize the breakdown of simpler physical theories, and the importance of psychosomatic concepts is just that they abandon the assumption that there must be a cart and a horse—that either mind must rule body or body mind. It proposes instead a more difficult assumption: more or less independent realities so correlated that, instead of a cart and a horse, we have two independent movers. Inject adrenalin into the blood stream and an animal will grow tensely apprehensive. If that were all we knew, then it might seem logical to assume that apprehension is "nothing but" adrenalin in the blood stream. But it is not all we know, since it is equally true that, if an animal become tensely apprehensive, adrenalin in unusual quantity will appear. Obviously something more than a simple, one-way relationship of cause and effect is involved. Body and mind are connected in some manner for which simple rationality has no name and which is difficult for it to conceive.

Perhaps, then, it will prove in general true that neither Platonic nor realist theories are adequate. Perhaps there is some sort of psychosomatic relationship which exists, not merely within the human body, but in the universe at large. Perhaps man is a microcosm in some sense more significant than that implied in medieval philosophy. Perhaps the whole human world of consciousness and value is related to the whole world of physical fact in some fashion analogous to that of the relationship between the soma and the psyche in the individual man.

If the mind may produce effects on the body as surely as the condition of the body can affect the mind, why should it be difficult to believe that, for example, a moral conviction may sometimes determine what will happen to a man just as surely as what has happened to him may sometimes determine what his moral conviction will be? Perhaps we are not compelled to choose between the belief that human beings are completely autonomous and the belief that all their mental experiences are physically determined. Perhaps both beliefs are incomplete. Perhaps both conduct and our conscious attitude toward it may, like the physical condition of the body, be determined either by society or the autonomous individual.

In almost every age there have been those who bewailed the corruption of manners, the decay of morality, the loss of standards, the prevalence of some moral disease. To that extent nearly all ages have been, like the present one, sometimes haunted by a sense of guilt as well as sometimes oppressed by anxiety. But if ours is, nevertheless, unusually anxious, it seems also more than usually convinced that some disease is epidemic. What professional moralists, professional preachers, and perhaps the querulous aged have always professed to believe is proclaimed today by a larger, more heterogeneous group. The young as well as the old frequently confess anxiety and a sense of some guilt which they do not know how to purge. That we are in some parlous state is often taken to be self-evident, even by those who agree on nothing else and who sometimes propose panaceas as irreconcilable as "return to God" on the one hand and Communism on the other. Seldom have doctors seemed to disagree more completely on everything except the fact that the patient is ill.

Behind the seeming completeness of this disagreement there lies, nevertheless, a common concern—from two irreconcilable points of view—with what we have called the human world of freedom and the importance of those illusions or realities which make up the realm of morals. To many political, sociological, and psychological "realists" it is the lingering persistence of our unscientific concern with this human world which is the cause of the disease. According to them what we need is to surrender the illusion completely and enter boldly upon that phase of social development which will begin when we have acknowledged without reservation the mechanical determinants of all human behavior; the unimportance of everything except behavior itself; and the meaninglessness of such concepts as honor, decency or fair play except as rationalizations of class interests. According to a minority of others, of course, what this first group calls the source of the disease is, on the contrary, the last protest of health against the morbidity which has all but destroyed it.

One thesis of this book seems therefore to receive support from both sides. The most general and inclusive account of the decision which our world is in the throes of making is that which describes it as an attempt to decide what attitude it will take toward all those phenomena which exist and have for so long existed in the consciousness—whatever may be their relation or lack of it to anything outside the human consciousness itself. In the simplest possible terms, the question is whether we have paid too little or too much attention to them; whether we have been too much or too little concerned with the failure of sociological and psychological accounts of the world in which we live either to satisfy us or to seem quite adequate to our immediate experience. If the answer to which we incline is "too little," then the problem becomes that of discovering how we might go about the business of paying more.

One solution which has today a respectable number of proponents is, of course, the simple "return to" God, religion, perhaps to the specific tenets of some historical Christian church. Another less often formulated than implied is merely the continuing search for some unified and scientifically based "world view" in which, for instance, the paradox of human bondage and human freedom is resolved by a science of psychology more adequate than that of any of the schools most popular today. The fact remains however that comparatively few either wish for or find possible any simple "return to," and that the science capable even of establishing any sort of comprehensible continuity between the phenomena of consciousness and those of matter seems a long way off. Meanwhile the consequences of our increasing tendency to dismiss as merely irrelevant whatever has not been incorporated into the so-called social sciences seem to many disastrous, to be in fact the ultimate cause of the anxiety and the hopelessness as well as of the disorder of our times.

At least one physical scientist, aware of the situation and at the same time professionally concerned with the fact that physics and chemistry have come to the point where they must accept the paradoxes that result from their inability to reconcile observed phenomenon with any consistent hypothesis concerning the nature of reality, has suggested the

THE FUNCTION OF DISCOURSE

possibility that the Science of Man should reconcile itself to analogous paradoxes. Thus President Conant, in the course of the same discourse that was previously quoted, does pass from an exposition of the situation in his own science to a very brief consideration of our moral crisis and he writes:

> Scientific theories . . . have little or no bearing on the age-old problem of good and evil. . . . Inquiries into the nature of this meaning would be inquiries about what I have called spiritual values.
>
> The dialectical materialists and also some agnostics would question whether the universe of inquiry I have just postulated is more than a name for mythology. . . . Almost certainly these people would maintain that advances in the social and biological sciences would eventually result in the final substitution of value judgments based upon science for those now accepted as part of our Judaic-Christian tradition, that it would be possible someday for psychiatry, social psychology, biology and anthropology to occupy this whole area of inquiry. Yet they would hardly challenge the statement that a vast number of value judgments today contain elements that have no connection with science. The question then appears to come down to this: Can those value judgments that do not now involve scientific concepts be replaced in principle by those that have originated in scientific investigations?
>
> As to the unifying, materialistic World Hypothesis, my doubt stems from its manifest inadequacy. . . . On the other hand, the formulations that attempt to include spiritual values, modern physics, biology, and cosmology within one total scheme attempt, to my mind, too much. . . . My preference would be for more adequate exploration of special limited areas of experience; one of these would include those experiences which can be ordered in terms of a system of spiritual values.

THE MEASURE OF MAN

So far as the present discourse is concerned the key sentence in this quotation is the last, and the key phrase is "adequate exploration of special limited areas of experience."

Metaphysics no less than science has, to be sure, unity as its ideal. The philosopher and the moralist, no less than the physicists, would like to eliminate all "limited areas" by extending his comprehension of each until the boundaries between them disappear. Einstein's increasingly inclusive "field theory" is a highly specialized illustration of the attempt in physical science to reduce the number of unique manifestations with which the scientist has to deal.

But the physical sciences have never refused to recognize or to investigate "limited areas" of physical phenomena when they could do no better. Physics and chemistry pursued their separate investigations until the very recent past when the boundaries between the two sciences were broken down. No one, to take an extreme example, ever proposed to disregard electricity until it could be shown, as Einstein has been attempting to show, that a generalized statement of the laws describing its operation is identical with a similarly generalized statement concerning gravity. But we are, on the other hand, faced with something not wholly unanalogous to such an absurdity when a psychologist or social scientist refuses to recognize as in any way significant the conscious phenomena which cannot be understood in terms of the concepts and methods of his mechanistic scheme. He insists on a unity which can be achieved only by disregarding what appear to others to be perfectly legitimate data.

When, at the beginning of this chapter, it was suggested that we might try the effect of refocusing our attention and of paying more rather than less attention to the realities of our conscious life, one intention was to suggest what President Conant implies in his dry and precise recommendation of a "more adequate exploration of special limited areas of experience." Such areas include some— like the whole area of sensations as distinguished from the physical cause of sensation—which only by the broadest definitions of the terms "can be ordered in terms of a system of spiritual values. But like "spiritual values" they also can be studied only if—and this is perhaps the most important fact of all—their ineluctable reality be admitted on the basis of the primary evidence of the consciousness rather than denied because they cannot be accounted for in some physical-chemical scheme. Moreover, if we do decide to study them as a real if limited area of experience, then we must do so in their own terms rather than in those borowed from sciences which, by definition, they do not concern.

What this means is that morality must be discussed in moral terms, and metaphysical questions, like the nature of value, in metaphysical. The "special limited areas of experience" cannot be adequately explored except by methods appropriate to, and on the basis of hypotheses consist-

ent with, the character of the area itself. We shall get nowhere if we insist on translating even the very terms of our
discussion into those appropriate only to some other special
limited area explored by a given science to which the very
existence of the consciousness is irrelevant. If, for example,
the areas covered by aesthetics and ethics are limited and to
some extent discontinuous areas, then they cannot be well
explored except by the acceptance of concepts and terms
similarly limited and similarly discontinuous with the concepts and terms which have been found most useful in
dealing with other limited areas. "Value" and even "Evil"
have significance for the organization of these areas even
though they cannot be defined in such a way as to be useful in any other.

In connection with this proposal it is certainly relevant
to remember that a "new psychology" sprang into being
when its founders boldly adopted a similar program. As
long as psychologists confined themselves to the investigation of phenomena which obviously lay within the area of
other sciences and dealt only in concepts regarded as legitimate by those exploring these other areas, their results were
singularly unimpressive. To read today about "Wundt's
Law" or even the vast palaver over such elementary things
as the distinction between perception and apperception—
in fact to read any pre-Freudian textbook—is to be oppressed by the triviality and aridity of the science as it then
existed and to realize that they were relieved only when a
William James permitted himself the liberty of reflecting

and moralizing in a fashion more in the tradition of Montaigne than in that of any formal science. Thus perhaps the most important of Freud's achievements was not the formulation of any of the specific theories associated with his name but simply the freedom which he won for psychology when he frankly introduced a novel set of concepts, beginning with that of the Psyche itself, and including the whole now familiar repertory of Suppression, Repression, Transformation, Transference, etc.

That he did so was, of course, the cause of much violent opposition on the part of the more orthodox. They accused him of merely inventing a mythology and demanded that he either demonstrate the neurological aspect of each of the penomenon he discussed, or in some way or other provide a means for translating his concepts into familiar ones. But Freud, however much he may have wished that such translation could be accomplished, recognized the reality of phenomena which could not be studied or discussed except in such terms as he invented. Here, in other words, was a limited area of experience which had to be either ignored or recognized both as limited and as to some extent discontinuous with the areas which physiological psychology explored.

Freud preferred not to disregard it. But there are many persons, including no doubt some by now reconciled to Freud, who will not recognize an analogous situation. They would rather deny the importance, the meaning, the very existence of limited areas of experience than examine them in terms of concepts foreign to whatever science they, as individuals, are professionally committed. They will not, for example, allow us to urge a pupil or a citizen to choose Good rather than Evil because they do not see how a machine can choose or how Good and Evil can be defined.

Even to enumerate the most important of the limited areas of experience which we tend to disregard and to suggest the terms and the concepts which might be employed in investigating them would require another volume as substantial as the present. One single example may, however, be given to illustrate what is involved and the kind of consequences which might result from a genuine study of such an area by methods which are, and to some extent were found in the past to be, genuinely fruitful.

The most obvious example of such an area is the area of morals. That such a realm exists and is of great importance has been taken for granted by most thinkers throughout most of human history. Traditionally it was discussed in terms of certain concepts like those of Right and Wrong, Individual Responsibility and the sense of Guilt or Innocence—all of which did, at least, correspond to something in conscious human experience and therefore appeared to be meaningful to those who entertained them. Without using these terms or some equivalents not yet invented no effective consideration can be given to the realm of morals as it presents itself to the conscious experience of the human being.

That the conclusions reached by those who did employ such terms varied greatly at different times and in different societies has been recognized at least since the time of Herodotus who anticipated Lecky's nineteenth-century *History of European Morals* by noting with wonder that what certain peoples regarded as a sacred duty appeared to others as an impiety of which they could not imagine themselves guilty. Yet most men at most times nevertheless still continued to believe either that different systems of morals were more or less valid attempts to formulate some True Morality or, at the very least, that they were rational formulations of a given set of mores without which those mores could not be successfully perpetuated.

To nineteenth-century science, on the other hand, it seemed evident that any area of so-called knowledge, or even any realm of discourse, within which no positive or generally accepted conclusions were reached was one upon which no time should be wasted, and science therefore proposed that the attention once given to moral questions should be devoted instead to the study of the objectively observable behavior which history records. Characteristically, the fact that this would involve the abandonment of all value judgments unless science itself could formulate them, was either overlooked or welcomed. So too and no less characteristically was the fact that the whole area of human experience within which the sense of Right and Wrong, of Guilt and Innocence, and of many other concomitants of conscious life are primary realities was dismissed as insubstantial or shadowy, and the human being was urged to accept a situation in which it becomes his duty to disregard, dismiss, even to feel ashamed of, some of the most vivid of his experiences.

Meanwhile, however, even science itself was compelled to recognize that conduct or behavior has important social consequences, and it soon found itself faced with the necessity of devising some way of dealing in its own terms with the problems which it took over when it dismissed as incompetent the moralist who had previously assumed responsibility for them. If social stability is impossible unless most men behave in accordance with some pattern, then you must discover what that pattern should be and you must find some sanctions for it, some method of persuading men to follow it. But, since no value judgments except those assumed to be self-evident could be invoked, the attempt to describe a desirable pattern of behavior had to lead to the statement that whatever has survival value is desirable and that nothing which cannot be shown to have such survival value is of any importance. And since no "moral sense" or any freedom to follow its dictates could be invoked, the method of promoting conformity to the pattern could not be other than of "conditioning."

Thus, if we follow this line, then, sooner or later, the ideal which we have to accept and the principles on which we must attempt to operate actually do come down to those described in *Walden Two*. Neither the ideal nor the methods used to realize it can be mitigated expect by the admission, recognized or unrecognized, of some sort of freedom for the individual and some sort of validity for value judgments other than those called self-evident.

Even supposing that such a society could survive—and we are already half way to it—it would be one in which the whole experience of living had become different from any formerly called human and, happily or unhappily, a large part of what has been the conscious life of the individual would have disappeared—as indeed some believe it is already tending to disappear in societies like our own where many admit, sometimes with distress, that they no longer can give intellectual assent to tastes, desires, impulses and reluctances which they have nevertheless not wholly succeeded in banishing from their consciousness. Thus even Communist revolutionaries sometimes confess that it is only after a struggle that they conquer moral scruples which they nevertheless believe to be scientifically indefensible.

But it is by no means yet certain that a society which believes in nothing except survival is actually capable of surviving; that the mere pragmatic usefulness and convenience of other ethical systems, even of very diverse sorts, are not such as to give them in practice a greater "survival value" than any general principles which could be accepted in such a society as that of Walden Two. It may very well be that those who believe in nothing but survival will always ultimately be conquered, or in some way superseded, by those who believe in something else.

Already in our own society we may find examples of the way in which the practical consequences of oversimplified concepts produce unfavorable results. Consider, for example, the result of the stress put on "objective studies" which confine themselves to behavior and resolutely refuse to concern themselves with any consideration of "what ought to be" as distinguished from what is. The subjects of such studies may be as diverse as what school children like to read, how diligently college students apply themselves, or, as in one notorious case, the sexual behavior of the human male. However accurate the information may be, the social scientist himself is committed to the opinion that it is meaningless unless this information is used for something, and we may well ask for what it is to be used.

Perhaps the sociologists will answer that we can use it in order to know what to expect. But in actual practice they are by no means always so neutral. Because thought about human problems can never get very far without reference to standards of some sort and because many sociologists have renounced all those which seem to them to imply an a priori value judgment, they almost inevitably begin soon to assume that "what is" must be the valid measure of "what ought to be" and that if we desire to find out either how diligently college students *should* study, or what the sexual conduct of the human male *should* be, we have only to find out to what extent the former actually do apply themselves and what the behavior of the latter usually is. Thus "right behavior" becomes identical with "normal" behavior, and "normal" comes

222

to mean simply "average." Hence, in a sense very different from what Aristotle intended, the mean becomes golden.

Obviously a moralist, or indeed anyone committed to any sort of belief that value judgments are legitimate, would object that to try to demonstrate what men ought to do by pointing out what they do do is to argue in an absurdly closed circle from which any consideration of the real point at issue is excluded. Certainly, they will say, it is hopeless to attempt to improve the moral condition of either the individual or society unless you assume that his behavior might be different from what it is.

Moreover, even those who reject completely the moralist's point of view ought to be able to see that the wide dissemination of the results of such studies is likely to have results which even they would recognize as highly undesirable. To most men the demands made on them by their parents, the society in which they live, the institutions with which they are connected, and even by their own consciousnesses, are to some extent burdensome, however light they may be by comparison with those which might be made. The college student who realizes that the less he does the less will be required of him is very likely to do less rather than more than what has hitherto been normal for him. The human male whose sexual behavior has been somewhat more restrained than the average is very likely to feel encouraged to relax his own standard. Thanks to both, to the student and to the mere male, the objective studies which will be made ten years hence will reveal that the average has been lowered still further and society will therefore expect less and less of its members who are pursuing the normal as it descends to lower and lower levels.

Perhaps a totalitarian society, sharply divided into the rulers and the ruled or—as it is sometimes more gently phrased—into the planners and the planned for, might well find use for secret investigations into the prevailing norms of behavior. But here is one more example of the fact that the premises and methods of one kind of "democracy" really require for their full justification not a democratic but a totalitarian society.

What, then, the program of the purely "objective" sociologist amounts to is the proposal that we should abandon, once and for all, that Moral Discourse which has gone on in Western civilization uninterruptedly for at least three thousand years. In justification of this proposal he argues that the Discourse has never reached objectively verifiable conclusions or produced measurable results. It has, as he says, "got us nowhere."

In reply it can nevertheless be said that it has got us the literature, the art, the philosophy, and the civilization which seem to many to be dying at last and that, unlike some objective sociologists, we are not glad to see it die. We can reply that the continuance of this civilization never has and does not now require that final conclusions should be reached; only that the Discourse should indeed go on; that what it accomplishes by its going on is not the definitive solution of any problem but the preservation of a state of mind in which an awareness that the problems are real is never absent for long. It is in Discourse of one kind or another—whether it be exposition, debate, artistic creation, or mere soliloquy—that the distinctively human aspects of conscious life manifest themselves. Without it they must inevitably fade away, and, unless that Discourse is "ordered in terms appropriate to the limited area of experience" with which it is concerned, it cannot exist.

When that Discourse which is the most characteristic result of conscious life is most aware of its moral purpose and when it pursues it most directly, then it takes the form of Ethics and the other branches of philosophy. But all the arts, including literature of course, are a possibly even more important part of the Discourse just because any given work of art is likely to deal with some particular, some very limited, area of experience and is free to explore it in even more specialized terms. Perhaps, indeed, the broadest possible definition of poetry would be that it is a report or analysis of some human experience ordered in terms of concepts involving a value judgment.

All the great novels and poems and plays take place in a universe which cannot be understood in "objective terms" and is meaningful only in the light of preferences based on the assumption that value judgments are valid. When we speak of those concerned with literature or the other arts as engaged in "humanistic studies" that is what our classification really implies. It means that the arts represent an attempt to organize human experience in terms

H

foreign to the physical or, for that matter, to all the would-be objective sciences, but peculiarly appropriate to the human experiences which elude those sciences. In its total effect the great body of art which civilization—or civilizations—has produced is Moral but not Moralizing. No specific moral system is deducible from it. Yet the experiences with which it deals are not meaningless even though they could not exist except in a universe of fact or imagination susceptible to organization in moral terms.

To submit oneself to the vicarious experience provided by any large and varied section of that body of art is not to learn any specific moral lesson or even to be taught to accept any given set of values. Almost every conceivable moral system and almost every conceivable system of value judgments have been used in one work or another as the basis of its organization. In a sense it might almost be said that the individual works cancel one another out at least as completely as the various formal religions and ethical philosophies do. For that reason moralists, in the narrow sense of the term, have often been suspicious of or even formally opposed to "humanistic" studies. But what one does learn by them is that the universe of human experience cannot be presented except in terms of *some* system of value judgments.

If the future of mankind really is to be, as many seem to suppose, one arranged and managed by "human engineers" who have achieved a unified theory of reality and developed a technique based on that theory by means of which certain results can be produced; if both that theory and that technique disregard as illusory and negligible the whole world of experience which cannot be ordered except in terms whose validity is not demonstrable in relation to anything except that world itself—then it would appear that this future must, to begin with, get along without whatever help civilizations of the past may have had from the stabilizing effect of accepted moral codes and must rely exclusively on the conditioning of the citizen by the techniques already developed.

But even this is only to begin with, for in that future the hitherto interrupted Discourse will have ceased and in its place there will remain only a discussion in the course of which the only questions ever to arise are those concerning techniques for producing results whose desirability is regarded as self-evident and therefore outside the range of profitable discussion. Art as we have known it will have ceased to exist because its only justification— namely as a form of Discourse in which, not the technique of survival, but the meaning of value judgments, with their consequence, is the central subject—will be regarded as no justification at all.

Conceivably such a society might be very much like that of Walden Two—except for the fact that in that utopia an improbable and functionless interest in the art and literature of the past is assumed to persist. But it is by no means certain that a society which had renounced Moral Discourse would be so innocuously agreeable as Walden Two. On purely a priori grounds a more brutal totalitarianism would seem at least as probable, and recent experience certainly seems to suggest that such totalitarian societies are the only ones actually coming into being or finding it possible to maintain themselves. We have seen the Nazi and the Communist states realize themselves before our eyes. No Walden Two exists except on paper.

Among those who are aware how logically the ideals of the totalitarian dictatorships follow from the premises of "today's thinking" we have already mentioned the conspicuous few who have come to the conclusion that only belief in God can arrest the progress of the trend—even, as they sometimes put it, that there is no halfway house between Roman Catholics and Communism. What their program involves is a very large order indeed and appears little likely to be filled within the narrow margin of time which seems all that is left to us. If we are to be saved it will probably be in some less dramatic fashion requiring a less abrupt reversal of the whole direction of thinking. Belief in the existence of a knowable God—to say nothing of a fixed universal theology—seems to most a long way off and dubiously attainable even in a remote future. If it really is essential to the preservation of what we think of as civilization then probably civilization will not be saved. But perhaps civilization can do with less.

This less it might do with was defined earlier in the present discussion as belief in the reality of a Minimal Man. The argument in the section now being concluded is that such a Minimal Man implies his willingness to participate in that Discourse which becomes possible as soon as he recognizes as significant the limited area of experience which constitutes conscious life and as soon as he consents to discuss it in relevant terms. It has been said also that the Minimal Man comes into existence at the moment when he does resume the Discourse and that doing so may put him back on the road which leads to the achievement of a human, as distinguished from an inhuman, society.

If the proposal that we should "return to God" seems to some impossibly ambitious, the counterproposal that we should simply begin to talk will certainly seem to others absurdly inadequate. How can anything so insubstantial as Discourse affect anything so substantial as the march of history or the operation of economic forces? Yet "mere talk," if it be actually part of the Discourse proposed, may have consequences greater than at first sight seem possible. Could, for example, any group of men have decided that hundreds of thousands of members of a particular ethnic group had better be systematically destroyed if those leaders had ever genuinely participated in any Discourse which recognized as valid the concepts around which the Discourse has usually revolved? Could the leaders of the Russian state have deliberately assumed as a primary premise that moral considerations have no place in political thinking if they had done the same? How can we effectively combat them unless we deny that "the end always justifies the means," or that there are no values other than those measurable in terms of survival and material goods? And how can we deny any of these things without recourse to the terms of Moral Discourse? Can we proceed to any other measures if we do not begin by recognizing the indispensability of such Discourse? How can we protest against inhumanity, treachery, ruthlessness, deceit and indecencies unless we believe that the opposite of each has some substantial reality? How can we object to the enslavement of mankind unless we assume that men are capable of freedom?

11

IT MAY NOT BE TOO LATE

That Discourse which began to falter several generations ago lost confidence in itself and lost therefore the power to protest effectively against an emerging world indifferent to all the values which the Discourse had tended to preserve. To resume it would require a good deal more than formal recognition of moral considerations and the function of philosophy. It would require also that we should learn again a habit of mind which acknowledges proudly rather than apologetically a loyalty to human values deeper than any other loyalty and a conviction that for us the universe of consciousness is the realest of all universes. That would, in its turn, mean an increased interest—indeed a different kind of interest—in those sections of the Discourse which art as well as philosophy record. It would mean, bluntly put, that we should again believe that what a Shakespeare has to say about human nature and human conduct is likely to be as true as, and rather more important than, what the summarizer of ten thousand questionnaires can tell us.

That most people do not now believe anything of the sort is obvious not only from the narrow definition they give to what they call "serious reading" but even more strikingly from certain trends in literature itself, many of which suggest that the writer is voluntarily renouncing his own special methods and ceasing to think of his work as part of the faltering Discourse; that he himself is often being won over instead to the convictions which dominate the thinking of the "objective sociologist."

This trend began to be evident in the nineteenth century when the "naturalists" who followed the lead of Zola began to speak of the ideal novelist as essentially a scientific student of society. To a degree which they perhaps did not fully realize this meant that they too had become convinced that the methods of science were the only methods capable of revealing any kind of truth; that "limited areas of experience" have ceased to exist; and that the whole unified area must be ordered in terms of one set of concepts.

Zolaesque positivism in the very simple form which it first assumed is no doubt rather old-fashioned today, but if one measures in terms of sheer bulk then the major part of recent serious prose fiction was produced by writers whose basic assumption is the same. The "problems" with which such fiction deals are those which occupy the sociologist, the politician, and the political theorist. Frequently its creators boast that their work is based on "observations" made in the spirit of the sociologist and that it suggests solutions deduced from sociological premises concerning "class interests," "social pressures," "group behavior," etc. Thus one of the most successful and esteemed of the very popular and at the same time "serious" contemporary novelists has confessed in connection with a discussion of one of his works that it could never have been written without a well-known sociological study of the milieu with which the novelist deals, and one needs no author's confession to realize that a very large part of contemporary fiction could not exist had the authors not based it on either the investigations of the sociologist or the case histories of the psychologist which have, for them, taken the place of both "imagination" and observation.

Such fiction serves no purpose and has no function except perhaps the very elementary one of presenting the sociologists' and the psychologists' material in a form palatable to those who have not sufficient seriousness of mind or sufficient capacity for sustained attention to read genuinely scientific works. Nothing new is contributed to our understanding of either man or society. In such cases what used to be called "the poet" is merely an amateur social scientist whose competence is usually no more than that expected of the amateur and one to whom the license of the poet has come to mean only a certain irresponsibility in dealing with material which the professional scientist treats responsibly. What he produces is very often analogous only to "the Henty books" of our youth. They put simplified history into a form palatable to the boyish understanding; he put sociology into a similar form for the benefit of the

H*

233

permanently immature. His novels are nothing except "educational," and they are very dubiously even that.

If it really is true that there is no area of experience which can profitably be investigated by methods other than those of the sciences, then the conclusion which ought to be drawn is not that literature must pass into the hands of amateur scientists but that it ought to disappear altogether—except perhaps as a method of propagating at a rather low level the conclusions of the social scientists. It can serve no other purpose because it can be no more than a duplication of effort undertaken, in this case, by a group not so well qualified as those engaged in the primary investigations. If, on the other hand, literature is to continue to exist as a somehow valuable form of Discourse, it can do so only by recognizing the validity of methods appropriate and peculiar to it and to the investigation of those areas of experience with which literature alone can deal effectively.

Some speak with contempt of this same "mere literature" whose superior achievements we are undertaking to celebrate. To them it seems obvious that literature as such is merely irresponsible and haphazard. It is less something which can even supplement the sciences than something merely prescientific in its aims and methods; something which uses incompetently if at all those techniques of observation, experiment, and accurate measurement which science has developed. At best they see it only as a diversion innocent in its effects only so long as we recognize it as the product of the childish rather than of the mature faculties of the mind. Only from the sciences themselves, so they say, can any trustworthy conclusions be drawn. We may amuse ourselves with the poets but we can learn only from the scientists.

Fortunately for them, none of those who assert the exclusive validity of measurement as the basis for conclusions seems to have noted how neatly the social scientists as a group have been hoisted on their own petard.

Faced recently with the problem of deciding what students in the colleges and universities should be temporarily exempt from military service, the United States government turned to the psychologists who provided a series of tests designed to measure the intellectual capacity of candidates for special consideration. Twenty fields of study were recognized and certain of the results of the tests, as reported in the *Publications of the Modern Language Association,* are startling indeed. Perhaps the sociologists and psychologists who designed the tests supposed that the largest proportion of superior men would be found studying in their fields, but the facts dramatically emphasize a contrary fact.

If the median scores made by college graduates on the Army General Classification Test are a reliable criterion our best brains go into the physical sciences, including engineering; our second best into law; and our third best into English. Students of psychology and economics not only rank below the students of English, but also below the students of the foreign languages. The social sciences (exclusive of history and economics) come still further down

—below biology, fine arts, nursing, history, agriculture and business. At the very bottom are, in this order, education, home economics, and physical education. Moreover, of the group composed of students whose grades fell within the range of the lowest twenty per cent of all graduate students tested, nearly one half were studying—education!

Champions of the humanities are privileged to doubt the accuracy of mental tests. But such tests can hardly be challenged by those who are responsible both for making them and for advocating that we should rely on the answers they provide. How then can they explain the fact that more of the superior minds (as measured by scientific methods) devote themselves to the study of literature (which is a prescientific activity) than to either psychology or the social sciences? How explain the further appalling fact that education has been falling more and more under the control of a group surpassed in intelligence by every other group except the two devoting themselves respectively to home economics and physical education?

If the figures are meaningful, then would it not be wise for society as a whole to consider more often what the most intelligent groups are learning rather than to accept so readily the plans and projects of the less intelligent? Yet there seems little evidence that either the public at large or some of the great foundations now financing study have any intention of doing so. According to another item in another issue of the *Publications* cited above, the Ford Foundation's 290 fellowships for the year 1953-54 were distributed as follows: social sciences 184; natural sciences and mathematics 48; literature, music and art 24; miscellaneous 34. Surely, if brains are to be subsidized, then it would be wise to subsidize the best brains most heavily.

As has already been suggested, the areas of experience with which only literature and the other arts can successfully deal are those which involve the consciousness rather than either mere behavior on the one hand or, on the other, the impersonal forces which are supposed by science to determine that behavior. The phenomena of this area can be successfully presented only when they are organized in terms of concepts which recognize the validity of value judgments. Hence literature as well as philosophy and all the other arts justifies its existence only when it finds some way of dealing with a kind of experience which the objective sciences must dismiss as outside their province, even when they do not deny its very existence as a significant reality. Art is successful only when we recognize ourselves in it, only when we are able to say, "This is indeed what living feels like." But no matter what our convictions may be, and even if we happen to be intellectually convinced that men are nothing but machines exhibiting conditioned behavior, we never recognize ourselves in a description of such creatures and never exclaim when we read it, "This is indeed what I have found my life to be like!" Even a behaviorist never seems to himself to be merely behaving, and even a statistician does not think of himself as a statistic.

Moreover, a literature which does justify its existence needs not only the terms and concepts necessary for the organization of the limited area with which it deals but needs also a corresponding series of terms and concepts—including, for example, the concept of "imagination"—which have to do with its methods rather than its materials. All of these necessary concepts are as elusive as the concept of value itself. Perhaps none of them has ever been very clearly defined, and to that extent the positivist is justified in his objection that when we invoke them we "do not know what we mean" in the sense that he knows what he means by, say, "experimental verification." But we cannot do without them nevertheless, because they refer, however imprecisely, to something very real and important. When we say, for example, that Shakespeare was gifted with an extraordinary imagination, we may not know exactly what we mean but we mean something which has never been more satisfactorily named, and it is far better to give it a possibly unsatisfactory name than to ignore its existence merely because we do not know a better one.

Attempts to explain what that term implies have varied all the way from the transcendental theories in which it is assumed that "imagination" is a primary "way of knowing" radically different from either inductive or deductive logic, to the rationalistic theories which, following the lead of Hobbes, explain it as merely the power of recombining images formed in the brain by sense impressions. Other even vaguer terms and concepts such as "poetic truth," "inner reality" and the rest are even more elusive and shifting. But their persistence testifies at least to the fact that the aims as well as the methods of art are distinguishable from those of science, and that "the poet" has seemed to perform some function which the scientist does not. Artists who have availed themselves of such terms have created works which do exhibit qualities different from those characteristic of writers who profess a positivistic philosophy, whether you want to designate these qualities by employing such terms as "ideality" and "higher truth" or not. Moreover and in any event, they are the qualities which art must exhibit if it is to be an effective part of that Discourse which we have been attempting to define. If the Discourse is to continue then the artists who participate in it must continue to use the old terms or find for them some equivalent.

In the case of each, as in the case of moral terms like "Right" and "Wrong," like "Obligation," "Duty," "Decency," and "Honor," the essential thing is not the word but the reality of the conscious experience which the word suggests. Conceivably all these words may fall into disuse. Possibly we shall someday find better ones. But it is supremely important that we should not forget or cease to interest ourselves in whatever reality lies behind them. Bernard Shaw, in those moments when he was aware of the dangers of the kind of "common sense" which he often defends, more than once denounced the modern tendency to "throw out the baby with the bath"; to forget, for example, when we reject the theology associated with the canonization of Joan of Arc, that behind the term "saint" lies the important fact that some human individuals really are capable of insights as well as deeds beyond the capacity of the usual human being, and that if we have no "modern" name for them then we had better still call them saints than forget the reality behind the concept of sainthood.

What a whole school of writers proposes to do when it follows the lead of the Science of Man is precisely "to throw out the baby with the bath." Because certain terms are not definable within the framework of its concepts it rejects not only the terms but the realities to which these terms do, however vaguely, refer. Within the limits of its framework Truth is Truth; Fact is objectively determinable Fact; and there is nothing else. If you cannot define Shakespeare's greatness or even demonstrate by any objective system of measurement that he is great, then to it there can be no meaning in the statement that he is.

To this kind of mind a given representation of human beings in action is either true to life or it isn't. A writer either tells the truth about man or he lies about him. And you cannot make a lie something else by calling it "idealism" or part of some "higher truth." Hence to anyone who takes this downright attitude there can be no such thing as "imagination" as distinguished from mere childish make-believe. A writer is a social scientist or he is nothing which can possibly be taken seriously. Thoreau, for instance, was merely talking nonsense when he declared that the business of art is not so much to imitate nature as to recover that original of which nature is itself an imitation.

Santayana was talking the same nonsense when he said that art is less concerned with repeating nature than with fulfilling her.

Obviously this is true, obviously neither Thoreau's nor Santayana's pronouncement can be other than nonsense, unless reality is more complex than those sciences which recognize only the objectively demonstrable believe. Perhaps indeed it can be said that Thoreau and Santayana really were talking nonsense unless the mind and the material world really are related in some psychosomatic fashion and are capable of influencing each other. But if reality does include the mind, then a literature which is concerned with imagination is contributing to reality, while one which recognizes only the truths of the physical, psychological and social sciences has ceased to be literature at all.

One way of illustrating one of the things which this may mean would be to point out that genuine literature is not merely an *account* of the world or of our life in it but also a significant *part* of it. This is true not only because art influences conduct—though it certainly does that—nor only because it teaches us to see more clearly and be more acutely aware of what the artists chose to see and to be aware of. It is a *part* rather than merely an *account* of the world and of our life in the world because it also furnishes a context as important, almost, as the context of nature itself.

The existence of literature is one of the things of which we are aware as we live our lives, and the fact that we have created it is one of the things which must be taken into account when human life is judged. Any estimate of the human universe and its meaning which does not take into account the fact that *Hamlet* and the "Ode on Intimations of Immortality" exist is bound to be as false as one which overlooked the fact that the sun shines, that flowers bloom and that men and women are sometimes happy. Any literature which, for any reason, however good it may seem, is not by its own creations increasing the number of things which make life more rewarding is failing, no matter how many truths of some sort it may be telling.

Everyone knows the Duc de la Rochefoucauld's famous remark that if it were not for poetry very few people would ever fall in love. That is a profound and true saying. What it means is that love and literature are very closely related inventions. But it is false to assume, as most of those who quote it seem to do, that it is the equivalent of admitting that what we call love "really is" only a biological urge dressed up in the insubstantial, lying fictions of a poet whose hypocrisy encourages the hypocrisy of others. Poetic experience is a fact as undeniably real as the biological urge. That few would ever fall in love if it were not for poetry is no truer than the converse: "If some men had not been able to fall in love no one would ever have written poetry." The fact that poetry exists is proof of the existence of love. There is no more justification for taking the hypothesis, "if there were no love," as equivalent to the statement, "There is no love," than there would be for saying, "If there were no sunlight there would be no green earth; therefore there really is no such thing as a leaf, and therefore a realist will never fail to make it clear when he has to describe a character who thinks he sees one that the whole thing is an illusion."

Obviously some large part of the difficulty of recognizing these facts stems from a definition of "reality" which is disastrously inadequate for the purposes of literature and for many other human purposes. In so far as the imaginative writer does anything more than present in a somewhat irresponsible manner the material and the conclusions more soberly dealt in by the scientist, he is able to do so because he has taken as his special subject the whole experience of living as it presents itself to certain individuals who seem to him important either because they are typical or, perhaps, because they are untypical. For him, at least, whatever is real in the mind is too real to be disregarded.

There may be a certain—though it is to me an inadequate—excuse for the exact scientist who refuses to consider as "real" for his purposes anything not objectively demonstrable. He may say that what he cannot measure, or weigh, or count, falls outside the real with which he can profitably concern himself. He may even say that so far as anything which his science can do about them they might just as well not exist. But he has no right to go the one step farther and say simply "Since for chemistry, or physics, or whatnot they do not exist, then we are compelled pragmatically to assume that they do not exist at all." He has no right to forget that the artist can take ef-

243

fective cognizance of much which he cannot. And though he may continue to function successfully in his profession while making his unjustifiable assumption, the imaginative writer who follows him in it destroys himself. One of the things which might be meant by the "ideality" of a writer is simply the extent to which he is aware of those things whose most obvious and perhaps only demonstrable reality is in the minds of men. Another might be the extent to which he has discovered or emphasized new manifestations of such things.

To put the whole thing in another way, one might say that the most important of all the functions of literature is to be a part of that whole Discourse whose function it is to prevent our understanding of the meaning of human life from degenerating into that "nothing but" to which all the sciences, because of the simplicity of their conceptions and the crudity of their instruments, tend to reduce it. Outside the sciences, if not within them, there is irrefutable evidence that, for instance, patriotism and the ideal of justice are not "nothing but" xenophobia and class interest. The last scene of Aeschylus' *Agamemnon* trilogy proves that men can love, and have loved, justice—just as *Romeo and Juliet* proves incontrovertibly that they have loved women. Few might ever have loved either if it were not for poetry. But poetry indubitably *is,* and many have learned how to love both.

By no means all contemporary literature aims, like that section of it we have been discussing, merely to illustrate orthodox sociology. In fact the writers most admired by those whose definite commitment is to literature are usually men who are in some kind of revolt against the whole materialistic optimism usually professed by the exponents of the Science of Man. Neither James Joyce nor D. H. Lawrence, to say nothing of Kafka or Rilke, or Eliot, would gladly accept citizenship in any Walden Two.

One whole school of contemporary poets escapes from sociology by proclaiming a new version of "art for art's sake" and retires into what is sometimes called a "world of words" where all the effects produced and the values sought are admitted to be discontinuous with what they themselves sometimes call "real life." Another school commits itself wholeheartedly to the irrational and seeks for the meaningful only in the universe of dreams, nightmares, delusions, obsessions and compulsions—as though only such disordered manifestations of mind were both sufficiently real in one sense and sufficiently unreal in another to justify treatment as a "limited area of experience" outside the province of the sciences; or as though the only escape from the logic of materialism were an escape into some kind of insanity.

Thus the very vehemence and extravagance of these revolts reveal the extent to which the concepts congenial to the social scientist have triumphed. The revolts themselves constitute a sort of confession that no rational opposition to such concepts is possible. If D. H. Lawrence—who seems to many the most *representative* modern writer—appeals to "dark" gods and "dark" spiritual values it is because he has been compelled to admit that only in darkness can they be found. James Joyce—to many the most *important* modern writer—takes as his theme the impossibility of achieving any rational reconciliation of the mean *facts* about man and his conduct with either his aspirations or the residual reality which may remain when religion, morality, or poetry are confronted with them. What we know of man and his world has, he seems to say, made it impossible any longer to attempt what Homer attempted. The only epic possible to us is not an epic in which human life can be represented as *corresponding* to anything noble, but only an epic in which it is *contrasted* with aspirations toward such nobility.

In some of the early novels of Aldous Huxley the situation was presented in its simplest form. A hero who has fallen romantically in love visits a biological laboratory where he sees a cock transformed into a hen by the administration of female hormones. He concludes, therefore, that chemistry is the reality behind all the most powerful passions, and that he is in the ridiculous position of centering his whole life around emotions and aspirations which could be made to disappear by a suitable course of hypodermic injections.

Quite rightly these novels never achieved the prestige of those by Joyce and Lawrence. In many respects they were what soon came to seem elementary and superficial. But because of that very fact they reveal clearly what lies behind the frustrations and dilemmas of writers in certain ways more gifted. The frustrations suffered by heroes of

Joyce and of Lawrence, no less than those of Huxley, arise out of the fact that they cannot reconcile the realities of their inner experience with the objective scientist's account of reality, and that, like almost all intelligent modern men, they are more inclined than they would like to be to accept the scientist's claim that his realities are in some way or another more substantial than those others which they nevertheless cannot and do not wish to dismiss as the mere lingering illusions the scientist declares them to be.

One result is that most modern writers who persist in the attempt to continue that Discourse of which literature has always been an important part do so in a fashion which is unhappy, desperate, and defeatist. What their writings suggest is that, if the Discourse is to continue at all, it must continue in ways which acknowledge defeat and can serve no purpose except as either a delaying action or an activity reserved exclusively for those who have managed a desperate escape from the pressures and convictions of mankind as a whole. The logical conclusion would be a world unequally divided between social scientists on the one hand and surrealists on the other.

A society like that of Walden Two except for the presence of a few neurotics carefully cultivating their obsessions and worshiping dark gods, might be preferable to one in which the inner life had entirely ceased. But it is not precisely what many would regard as ideal. Surrealism, like aestheticism, recognizes limited areas of experience, but they are both too limited and too completely discontinuous with all other areas to serve as the only remaining subject of whatever significant Discourse is not practical and scientific. The values which we most need to rediscover are not those of an irrational but of a rational area, and meaning needs to be found in what can be rationally organized not in what cannot. We have all but given up the cultivation of our gardens; when we concern ourselves at all with the realm of consciousness it is usually only to explore our wilderness instead.

A machine which can sometimes go crazy is hardly a satisfactory substitute for a Minimal Man. If we ever discover him again it will be because we have been able to oppose the reality of a rational mind to the reality of the objective world of phenomena; because we have learned again not merely to recognize the universe of consciousness but have learned to organize our Discourse concerning it in appropriate terms.

To a good many students of contemporary literature the late André Gide was coming to displace James Joyce as the representative man of letters for our generation, and Gide was certainly no surrealist on the one hand and no sociologist *manqué* on the other. Of him it might indeed be said that his central aim was to take part in that Discourse which we have been trying to understand. Yet it is equally clear that in his books the Discourse continues to go round and round a closed circle largely because, like so many anthropologists and sociologists, he was convinced that Good and Evil cannot possibly mean anything more than "according to some set of habits and customs." If you believe that morals are no more than mores, then you may either conclude that the good life consists in complete "adjustment" to the prevailing mores or, like Gide, that the individual may claim unlimited license.

As Justin O'Brien's *Portrait of André Gide* and Martin du Gard's *Recollections of André Gide* have recently made clear, Gide's relativism, combined with his determinism, made it possible for him to defend any action by saying simply, "I am what I am and must do what I do." As he remarked on one occasion, "I have ceased to believe in sin," and he managed with unintentional adroitness to reduce to parody what might have been a rational protest against the fanatical insistence on "normality" and "health" by writing, "Health does not seem to me such an enviable possession. It is merely an equilibrium, a state of mediocrity in everything. . . . A humpback is a man plus a hump, and I prefer that you should look upon health as a deficiency of disease." At such a moment as this, he approaches surrealism because surrealism is the only possible escape from an acceptance of some such definition of the good life as is proposed in *Walden Two* unless one is able to reject, as Gide was not, the premises on which the definition rests.

Undoubtedly he presents one of the most admirable aspects of the modern spirit when he seeks to be Free, to be Sincere, and to discover his Real Self. But the nearer he seemed to come to reaching any of his goals, the more clearly he seemed to discover, not one of those stable absolutes which it has been the best dream of mankind to glimpse, but some relativity, some delusion, or some vacuum. What does his "Sincerity" enable him to confess except what has usually been thought to be shameful? What does the "Real Self" turn out to be except a welter of conflicting impulses in the face of which it is possible to say only that I must do what I do and that good and evil are one? What does "Freedom" come down to in the end except the possibility of committing that *acte gratuite* which is the *reductio ad absurdum* of free will? If Gide is the most representative modern writer, then modern literature has found it impossible to make any reply to the proponents of a pragmatic, utilitarian, instrumentalist, materialistic and norm-worshiping civilization, except by insisting on the fanatical cultivation of opposite extravagances.

To acknowledge the failure of contemporary literature is not to discover an easy way out of a desperately complex situation. A literature which falters is merely a part of the whole humane Discourse which, as a whole, is faltering. If our decreasing ability to comprehend either private or public life in humanly meaningful terms tends to be decreased still further by the novels and poems we read, it is equally true that the decreasing ability is one of the reasons why the fiction writer and the poet feel compelled to address us in terms which we can understand. Cause cannot be clearly separated from effect or symptom from disease. Each becomes in turn the other.

The citizen cannot shift the responsibility to the artist, nor the artist shift it to the citizen. They are unfortunate, or unwise, or guilty, together. To say to the poet merely

"Be noble" is as naïvely preposterous as to say to the citizen no more than "Be good." The one is no more likely to produce mere hypocrites than the other to produce artistic insincerity. Though the best writers today are not quasi sociologists, neither are they the pseudoheroic and the pseudo noble. More often they are actually the most "modern" in the sense of being the most obscure and the most despairing. But they are not either because obscurity and despair are good things in themselves—only because sincerity is a good thing in itself and the artist has succumbed very much as the citizen has succumbed to the grand strategy of recent intellectual life.

Hardly less than the citizen he needs to be rescued, and the most that can be asked of either him or the citizen is some realization of the plight of both and some effort to discover a means of escape from it.

Not long ago a distinguished American novelist accepted the Nobel Prize in a speech which astounded his readers by its idealism and by his expression of faith in the future of Man as a moral being. Nothing suggested that either this idealism or this faith was the product of any recent conversion. On the contrary what the speaker seemed to be saying was that they were in part at least what his novels had been intended to convey. Yet most of his readers had never suspected anything of the sort. At some point the failure of communication had been so complete that they had not, to put it in the simplest terms, known "what side he was on."

Whatever the explanation of this fact may be, the fact

is appalling. Here was a voice raised in protest against the system of beliefs from the effects of which a civilization is dying. Here was a very gifted man attempting in his own way to reanimate the faltering Discourse. Yet few were aware even of his intention. Was this because it has become almost impossible for anyone to say clearly what he wants to say? Or was it because we have so completely accepted the assumption that a good writer is necessarily "on the other side" that we simply could not hear what this one was telling us? Was it, even, because the writer himself, aware of the public distrust of anyone who defends even indirectly the case for supposing that man could be noble, deliberately concealed his convictions? In any event a successful career had been, so far and in this one sense, a failure.

If this attempt to analyze and comment on certain aspects of a modern temper finds any sympathetic audience, that audience will certainly not include various large sections of contemporary opinion. Obviously it cannot include those who are committed to the belief that man is essentially nothing but a machine capable of conditioned behavior and who look forward with complacency to a society frankly based on this assumption. Equally obviously it cannot hold for long those who reject mechanistic and deterministic theories but who find in some formal religious creed what they believe to be not only a satisfactory alternative but the only alternative possible.

To neither of these groups can anything further be said.

Indeed most members of either will have ceased long before this to follow what has been said already. Hence these concluding words must be addressed not to them but those readers who have followed the discussion with a certain degree of sympathy but to whom the practical conclusions to be drawn seem vague and unsatisfactory.

Such readers will be neither complacently "modern" nor securely at rest in some sure faith. They will neither like nor quite believe what they have been most often told by their contemporaries about the nature of man, about the character of the good life, and about the methods most likely to assure that good life for the men of the future. But they will doubt whether anything can be done about the fact that this future does, indeed, seem to belong to those with whom they disagree; doubt especially, that if anything can be done it is likely to be through activities as elusive as metaphysics, moral discourse, and art.

They are ready enough to grant that dialectic materialism, for instance, probably is not a completely adequate explanation of the whole of the human achievement; that value judgments other than those self-evidently based on survival as the *summum bonum* have some kind of meaning; that preference and choice are sometimes and to some extent not merely the effects of an environment, but factors which are capable of modifying it. But they still believe that there is so large an element of truth in what they reject as the whole truth, still believe that men are so largely the product of their conditioning, as inevitably to doubt the effectiveness of an attempt to modify significantly the course of history by any method which relies, even to an important extent, on the human will, the human imagination, and in general on whatever freedom is possible within a restricted realm.

In short, though to some extent they accept the account which has been given of the modern temper and to some extent agree that certain very undesirable social and intellectual phenomena accompany it, they are very much inclined to doubt that the phenomena can be controlled by means of the convictions which go along with them. Without quite insisting that such convictions are "nothing but" symptoms of a process under way, they are by no means sure that there is any way of dealing with them that does not accept them as, for all practical purposes, hardly more than that. It is easy for them and for all of us to believe that a man may be "the product of" any one of a number of external "forces." When we are told that he, or the group to which he belongs, is thus or so because of "economic conditions," or "social conventions," or "early conditioning," or even "psychic traumas," it seems to us probable enough. The one thing which we find it hard to believe is that what he might be "the product of" is himself. For such dubious readers it may be worth while to state what attitude the author of the present discussion takes toward their doubts.

He has not, it should be said at once, any disposition merely to brush them aside. If man has always been partly the creator and partly the creature of his total environment; if he has always been partly what he was made as

254

well as partly what he made himself—then it may seem that the very developments which we have been describing must mean that the balance is less in favor of the autonomous, creative side of his nature than it ever was before. If some men have mastered to a degree never before approached the techniques for exploiting the mechanical, predictable, and controllable side of man's nature, it may seem hopeless to try to oppose to them forces which, on their part, have, if anything, grown weaker rather than stronger.

Moreover, if those individuals in whom the human spirit is conspicuously stronger than the conditioned reflex are less numerous than those concerning whom the contrary must be admitted, and if the new methods of organizing majorities make these majorities more powerful than they ever were before, then it may seem that the engineers must achieve their ultimate aims and prove that they can, as they sometimes assume, successfully ignore even when they do not deny the existence of all forces which they cannot use for their purpose. As the Frazier of *Walden Two* insisted, he does not have to prove that man can never be free; it is enough for him to demonstrate that he can operate successfully—according to his definition of success—by disregarding whatever autonomy the individual may be capable of.

It has sometimes been suggested that those who would prefer a world different from that which the Fraziers seem determined to develop should themselves attempt to seize the instruments of propaganda and the whole machinery for "conditioning"—much as the Communists seized the instruments of production. But one cannot do that without betraying one's own cause; one can hardly use the methods of the enemy without accepting more of his premises than we can afford to accept. What we have to offer seems potentially less effective than even the dogmatic faith of the religious convert or the finished code of morals which often goes with a religion. To say that the world could be saved by a solution of its moral problems would sound unconvincing enough to most people. What we are proposing seems even less promising. What it comes down to is salvation, not through the solution of the problems of morality, but through the mere recognition that they exist.

Yet one must start somewhere if one is to start at all, and the whole trend of this discussion has been to suggest that there is no other place to start. Grant the premise, either that human freedom does not exist or even that it is too limited to be worth taking into account, and there is no breaking the chain of logic which leads ultimately to the position of the most extreme proponents of "human engineering" as the only method of dealing with man or his problems. Grant his contentions and there is no breaking the chain which leads in its turn to some sort of totalitarian society. If, on the other hand, everything which has been or ever will be was not fixed and inevitable from the dawn of creation, then it must be because of either a random element in the universe or because an effective freedom to choose exists somewhere. And there seems no more likely place where it might reside than in man himself. If he is to use this freedom actually to move the world, if he is not merely to be moved by it, then he must have some point outside the world of the physically and mentally determined on which to rest his lever. That fulcrum cannot be anything except "values" deliberately chosen.

Thus, however limited human freedom may be, the freedom, if it exists at all, is unique, and, given a lever with which to operate, there is no guessing how powerful a force the free man may exert. To say this is not to say that rulers, educators, publicists, and social workers should henceforth rely on nothing except man as a free moral agent and therefore on his power to choose his values and govern his conduct. But it does mean that they must not leave any of these things out of account.

Because the human intelligence is weak, and because the pressure of events is always forcing it to choose some method and some principle for dealing with its problems, it is perpetually tempted to simplify too much. One of the simplifications to which it is especially prone is that which attempts to avoid the distinction between the *sine qua non* and "the one thing necessary." But the distinction is vital here as so often it is. Belief in the reality of values and in man's ability to recognize or to establish them is a *sine qua non* for any world which is to remain what has previously been thought of as human. It is not, however, all that is necessary for the management of such a world.

Five thousand years of history demonstrate how far noble ideas, exalted faiths, and stern codes of morality are

I

257

from actually guaranteeing wise, just, or even decent conduct. Obviously, these ideals and codes are not enough; despite them, human history has seemed to some no more than a record of crimes and follies. Men who profess, sometimes sincerely, to put honor above everything have by no means always acted honorably. But it is no less true that it is because of what some men have professed, and to some extent been influenced by, that human history is not "nothing but" crimes and follies.

Past history shows that beliefs and professions are not all that is necessary. It shows also that the other necessary things include more than that sincerity and consistency which were lacking often enough. These "other things necessary" include intelligence and knowledge, and knowledge includes much of what we know about science and technology. But the lesson of the most recent history is something quite different from that of the past. It is that the thing we have recently neglected is also a *sine qua non*.

How else can one explain the fact that, knowing so much more than our forefathers knew, and having, possibly, even more good will than they, we should nevertheless be failing so conspicuously; failing even to the point of coming sometimes to doubt that we are good enough to survive or that our problems are solvable? If, on our premises, they seem not to be, then a very good case is emerging for the contention that a time has come for trying others.

Unless something of the kind is possible, then we really are helpless, no matter how much we may talk about "planning" or "intervening in the process of evolution." Just as the ideal of a "free society" is absurd unless individuals are somehow free, so, even more obviously, we cannot "plan" if what we think we are planning is actually only the inevitable result of what has already happened. Unless the unpredictable and the undetermined is possible, then the society which we talk about "building" is actually being built willy-nilly and all our resolutions and efforts are the mere illusions which some Marxists seem to assume that they are. As one of them is reported to have admitted in the course of a debate in the Soviet Union, it is highly unphilosophic even to urge: "Workmen of the world, unite!" The most that can reasonably be said is merely: "The workmen of the world are uniting."

Some may be hearty enough to reply that evolution—or the dialectic of matter, if they prefer to call it that—has done pretty well by us so far, and that they are content to trust the future to it. So far, they think, it has led us upward and onward. Why doubt that it will continue to do so?

Actually there is no real assurance that it will unless we surrender to it our own hopes and desires and define "upward and onward" to mean no more than whatever changes may take place. There is certainly no assurance that a mechanically evolving universe will move in any direction which we, by our present standards, regard as

259

desirable. Indeed a very pretty case could be made out for the contention that it is actually headed in a contrary direction.

Leaving Man out of account for the moment, we observe that the most recent plants are the members of that composite family which include many of the most pestiferous weeds. The "highest" insects—*i.e.,* the most recent—are the group to which the ant belongs. By the criterion proposed by Professor Skinner—prolonged and flourishing survival—these two classes of organisms are the most successful of living creatures. Yet the composites have achieved their success partly because they have learned to produce a prodigious number of seeds without wasting much strength in the production of flowers. More obviously the ants have achieved theirs because they have solved their social problem so perfectly that they do not even need to practice the techniques for "conditioning." They are born properly conditioned, and they would no doubt argue, if they were capable of arguing, that a reflex which has become fixed by heredity is "higher" than one which must be impressed by society upon each new individual.

Taking their condition as evidence, it would seem that the ultimate condition to which evolution tends is that of a dull and even hideous efficiency. And if to some it seems that human society is tending in that direction, then it is not really fantastic to suggest that the cases are parallel and that the few thousand years which are to us the history of human civilization actually constitute no more than a brief interlude of inefficiency which intruded between the time when the nervous system of the human animal reached a certain unprecedented degree of complexity and the time—now approaching—when that complexity will achieve a more stable organization and all the phenomena associated with what we call civilization will disappear.

If the true situation is anything like that, then the disappearance of man's belief in his own autonomy will signalize a decisive crisis in the course of evolution. All that part of the human past which we know anything about then represents the phase of development during which the delusion that he is more than a machine influenced the character of his conditioning and was one of the factors of which he was a product. The future will be that accelerating phase during which this factor no longer operates. Gradually he will be conditioned to accept the fact that he is nothing in himself, and even the epiphenomena associated with consciousness and the delusions regarding choice and value will disappear.

Perhaps they have already begun to do so. Perhaps there is nothing which can alter or even delay the process. But if the so-called epiphenomena are actually something more, if the very ability to imagine that we may be something more than "products" is something new in the universe and something which corresponds to a reality, then we may be having our last chance to make something of it. We should think twice before we consent to dismiss the possibility from our minds. If we do not, we may never be able really to think again.